WITHDRAWN

Juvenile Justice

POINT
COUNTERPOINT

Juvenile Justice

David L. Hudson Jr.

SERIES EDITOR
Alan Marzilli, M.A., J.D.

CHELSEA HOUSE
PUBLISHERS
An imprint of Infobase Publishing

Juvenile Justice

Copyright © 2010 by Infobase Publishing

All rights reserved. No part of this book may be reproduced or utilized in any form or by any means, electronic or mechanical, including photocopying, recording, or by any information storage or retrieval systems, without permission in writing from the publisher. For information, contact:

Chelsea House
An imprint of Infobase Publishing
132 West 31st Street
New York, NY 10001

Library of Congress Cataloging-in-Publication Data
Hudson, David L., 1969-
Juvenile justice / by David L. Hudson, Jr., Alan Marzilli.
p. cm. — (Point/counterpoint)
Includes bibliographical references and index.
ISBN 978-1-60413-508-4 (hardcover)
1. Juvenile justice, Administration of—United States—Juvenile literature. I. Marzilli, Alan. II. Title. III. Series.
KF9779.H83 2009
345.73'08—dc22

                    2009029616

Chelsea House books are available at special discounts when purchased in bulk quantities for businesses, associations, institutions, or sales promotions. Please call our Special Sales Department in New York at (212) 967-8800 or (800) 322-8755.

You can find Chelsea House on the World Wide Web at http://www.chelseahouse.com.

Text design by Keith Trego
Cover design by Alicia Post
Composition by EJB Publishing Services
Cover printed by Bang Printing, Brainerd, MN
Book printed and bound by Bang Printing, Brainerd, MN
Date printed: March 2010
Printed in the United States of America

10 9 8 7 6 5 4 3 2 1

This book is printed on acid-free paper.

All links and Web addresses were checked and verified to be correct at the time of publication. Because of the dynamic nature of the Web, some addresses and links may have changed since publication and may no longer be valid.

FOREWORD ||||▷

Alan Marzilli, M.A., J.D.
Birmingham, Alabama

The POINT/COUNTERPOINT series offers the reader a greater understanding of some of the most controversial issues in contemporary American society—issues such as capital punishment, immigration, gay rights, and gun control. We have looked for the most contemporary issues and have included topics—such as the controversies surrounding "blogging"—that we could not have imagined when the series began.

In each volume, the author has selected an issue of particular importance and set out some of the key arguments on both sides of the issue. Why study both sides of the debate? Maybe you have yet to make up your mind on an issue, and the arguments presented in the book will help you to form an opinion. More likely, however, you will already have an opinion on many of the issues covered by the series. There is always the chance that you will change your opinion after reading the arguments for the other side. But even if you are firmly committed to an issue—for example, school prayer or animal rights—reading both sides of the argument will help you to become a more effective advocate for your cause. By gaining an understanding of opposing arguments, you can develop answers to those arguments.

Perhaps more importantly, listening to the other side sometimes helps you see your opponent's arguments in a more human way. For example, Sister Helen Prejean, one of the nation's most visible opponents of capital punishment, has been deeply affected by her interactions with the families of murder victims. By seeing the families' grief and pain, she understands much better why people support the death penalty, and she is able to carry out her advocacy with a greater sensitivity to the needs and beliefs of death penalty supporters.

The books in the series include numerous features that help the reader to gain a greater understanding of the issues. Real-life examples illustrate the human side of the issues. Each chapter also includes excerpts from relevant laws, court cases, and other material, which provide a better foundation for understanding the arguments. The volumes contain citations to relevant sources of law and information, and an appendix guides the reader through the basics of legal research, both on the Internet and in the library. Today, through free Web sites, it is easy to access legal documents, and these books might give you ideas for your own research.

Studying the issues covered by the POINT/COUNTERPOINT series is more than an academic activity. The issues described in the books affect all of us as citizens. They are the issues that today's leaders debate and tomorrow's leaders will decide. While all of the issues covered in the POINT/COUNTERPOINT series are controversial today, and will remain so for the foreseeable future, it is entirely possible that the reader might one day play a central role in resolving the debate. Today it might seem that some debates—such as capital punishment and abortion—will never be resolved.

However, our nation's history is full of debates that seemed as though they never would be resolved, and many of the issues are now well settled—at least on the surface. In the nineteenth century, abolitionists met with widespread resistance to their efforts to end slavery. Ultimately, the controversy threatened the union, leading to the Civil War between the northern and southern states. Today, while a public debate over the merits of slavery would be unthinkable, racism persists in many aspects of society.

Similarly, today nobody questions women's right to vote. Yet at the beginning of the twentieth century, suffragists fought public battles for women's voting rights, and it was not until the passage of the Nineteenth Amendment in 1920 that the legal right of women to vote was established nationwide.

What makes an issue controversial? Often, controversies arise when most people agree that there is a problem but disagree about the best way to solve it. There is little argument that poverty is a major problem in the United States, especially in inner cities and rural areas. Yet, people disagree vehemently about the best way to address the problem. To some, the answer is social programs, such as welfare, food stamps, and public housing. However, many argue that such subsidies encourage dependence on government benefits while unfairly penalizing those who work and pay taxes, and that the real solution is to require people to support themselves.

American society is in a constant state of change, and sometimes modern practices clash with what many consider to be "traditional values," which are often rooted in conservative political views or religious beliefs. Many blame high crime rates, and problems such as poverty, illiteracy, and drug use on the breakdown of the traditional family structure of a married mother and father raising their children. Since the "sexual revolution" of the 1960s and 1970s, sparked in part by the widespread availability of the birth control pill, marriage rates have declined, and the number of children born outside of marriage has increased. The sexual revolution led to controversies over birth control, sex education, and other issues, most prominently abortion. Similarly, the gay rights movement has been challenged as a threat to traditional values. While many gay men and lesbians want to have the same right to marry and raise families as heterosexuals, many politicians and others have challenged gay marriage and adoption as a threat to American society.

Sometimes, new technology raises issues that we have never faced before, and society disagrees about the best solution. Are people free to swap music online, or does this violate the copyright laws that protect songwriters and musicians' ownership of the music that they create? Should scientists use "genetic engineering" to create new crops that are resistant to disease and pests and produce more food, or is it too risky to use a laboratory to create plants that nature never intended? Modern medicine has continued to increase the average lifespan—which is now 77 years, up from under 50 years at the beginning of the twentieth century—but many people are now choosing to die in comfort rather than living with painful ailments in their later years. For doctors, this presents an ethical dilemma: should they allow their patients to die? Should they assist patients in ending their own lives painlessly?

Perhaps the most controversial issues are those that implicate a Constitutional right. The Bill of Rights—the first 10 Amendments to the U.S. Constitution—spells out some of the most fundamental rights that distinguish our democracy from other nations with fewer freedoms. However, the sparsely worded document is open to interpretation, with each side saying that the Constitution is on their side. The Bill of Rights was meant to protect individual liberties; however, the needs of some individuals clash with society's needs. Thus, the Constitution often serves as a battleground between individuals and government officials seeking to protect society in some way. The First Amendment's guarantee of "freedom of speech" leads to some very difficult questions. Some forms of expression—such as burning an American flag—lead to public outrage, but are protected by the First Amendment. Other types of expression that most people find objectionable—such as child pornography—are not protected by the Constitution. The question is not only where to draw the line, but whether drawing lines around constitutional rights threatens our liberty.

The Bill of Rights raises many other questions about individual rights and societal "good." Is a prayer before a high school football game an "establishment of religion" prohibited by the First Amendment? Does the Second Amendment's promise of "the right to bear arms" include concealed handguns? Does stopping and frisking someone standing on a known drug corner constitute "unreasonable search and seizure" in violation of the Fourth Amendment? Although the U.S. Supreme Court has the ultimate authority in interpreting the U.S. Constitution, its answers do not always satisfy the public. When a group of nine people—sometimes by a five-to-four vote—makes a decision that affects hundreds of millions of others, public outcry can be expected. For example, the Supreme Court's 1973 ruling in *Roe v. Wade* that abortion is protected by the Constitution did little to quell the debate over abortion.

Whatever the root of the controversy, the books in the POINT/ COUNTERPOINT series seek to explain to the reader the origins of the debate, the current state of the law, and the arguments on either side of the debate. Our hope in creating this series is that readers will be better informed about the issues facing not only our politicians, but all of our nation's citizens, and become more actively involved in resolving these debates, as voters, concerned citizens, journalists, or maybe even elected officials.

Although juvenile arrest rates have dipped in the United States in recent years, in 2007 there were still nearly 2.2 million arrests involving people under the age of 18. While crimes such as under-age drinking and vandalism—which make up a significant portion of these arrests—have a negative impact on society, the public and the courts are often more willing to grant leniency to youths who commit such offenses. The thinking behind such lenient sentences is that these juveniles can learn from their mistakes, particularly if they are required to perform community service or engage in some other form of "character-building" punishment. Perhaps based on the flex-ibility offered by the juvenile justice system, a smaller percentage of youthful offenders are having their cases heard in criminal courts.

Many people believe that true justice requires that some minors be tried in adult courts, because those who have already earned long "rap sheets" and have often progressed to violent crimes, includ-ing murder, commit many of these crimes. Although a divided U.S. Supreme Court recently held that execution of juvenile offenders is no longer permissible, many have criticized the decision. However, voices have already begun to unite against the alternative to execu-tion, life in prison without the possibility of parole.

An Overview of Juvenile Justice

The trouble with all our work in the criminal law is that we pay more attention to the act than to the cause of the act. Our chief concern with the lawbreaker is, "What did you do?" whereas it should be, "Why did you do it?" Nobody—man or boy, woman or girl, breaks a law just for the fun of doing it. There is a reason for all the acts that we call crimes. It seems to me that the only preventative for an act of that kind is to find out the cause and remove it, instead of inflicting punishment for the crime. . . . We may begin to hope when we adapt to men the Juvenile Court system of overcoming evil with good.

—Judge Benjamin Lindsey[1]

The juvenile justice system in the United States has developed and shifted markedly in a little more than 200 years of American history. Throughout the seventeenth and much of the eighteenth centuries, juvenile offenders were treated with harshness and subjected to imprisonment. In the late 1800s and early 1900s, however, society witnessed the beginning of the Progressive Era. Progressives advocated a broad range of economic, moral, political, and social reforms in response to the changes brought about by industrialization. In 1899, Cook County, Illinois, introduced the first juvenile court. In July of that year, Judge Richard S. Tuthill sent 11-year-old Henry Campbell, charged with stealing, to live with his grandmother in upstate New York. The judge believed that Campbell might benefit from a fresh start in a rural environment.[2] Tuthill was known as "the father of the juvenile court."[3]

Another pioneer in the Progressive era and a true champion of juvenile rights was Judge Benjamin Lindsey of Denver. The *New York Times* referred to him as the "pioneer apostle of the Juvenile Court."[4] The *Atlanta Constitution* referred to Lindsey's juvenile court as "the model juvenile court in the world."[5] Lindsey traveled the country to encourage his colleagues in other states to create juvenile courts that would be focused on the idea of rehabilitating young people: "The problem of the child is the problem of the State; and the Juvenile Court would substitute the detention school for the jail, and thus correct and protect the child."[6] Lindsey's court had a tremendous effect on his community and elsewhere in the United States. The recidivism rate for youths appearing in his juvenile courtroom was low. As Lindsey said, "It is cheaper and wiser to save the children than to punish the criminals."[7]

The effect of the juvenile court was momentous. In the two years before the juvenile court's establishment, more than 1,700 juveniles were sent to adult prisons. In the two years after the passage of the law that led to the court's creation, 60 juveniles were sent to prison.[8] Instead, the youths were given options more suited to treatment and rehabilitation. It was an era in which many in society believed in ferreting out the best interests of children and treating them with compassion. Author Steven

FROM THE BENCH

Kent v. United States, 383 U.S. 541, 556 (1966)

While there can be no doubt of the original laudable purpose of juvenile courts, studies and critiques in recent years raise serious questions as to whether actual performance measures well enough against theoretical purpose to make tolerable the immunity of the process from the reach of constitutional protection to adults. There is much evidence that some juvenile courts, including that of the District of Columbia, lack the personnel, facilities and techniques to perform adequately as representatives of the State in a *parens patriae* capacity, at least with respect to children charged with law violation. There is evidence, in fact, that there may be grounds for concern that the child receives the worst of both worlds: that he gets neither the protections accorded to adults nor the solicitous care and regenerative treatment postulated for children.

This concern, however, does not induce us in this case to accept the invitation to rule that constitutional guaranties which would be applicable to adults charged with the serious offenses for which Kent was tried must be applied in juvenile court proceedings concerned with allegations of law violation. The Juvenile Court Act and the decisions of the United States Court of Appeals for the District of Columbia Circuit provide an adequate basis for decision of this case, and we go no further. . . .

It is clear beyond dispute that the waiver of jurisdiction is a "critically important" action determining vitally important statutory rights of the juvenile. The Court of Appeals for the District of Columbia Circuit has so held. See *Black v. United States*, supra; *Watkins v. United States*, 119 U.S. App. D.C. 409, 343 F.2d 278 (1964). The statutory scheme makes this plain. The Juvenile Court is vested with "original and exclusive jurisdiction" of the child. This jurisdiction confers special rights and immunities. He is, as specified by the statute, shielded from publicity. He may be confined, but with rare exceptions he may not be jailed along with adults. He may be detained, but only until he is 21 years of age. The court is admonished by the statute to give preference to retaining the child in the custody of his parents "unless his welfare and the safety and protection of the public can not be adequately safeguarded without . . . removal." The child is protected against consequences of adult conviction such as the loss of civil rights, the use of adjudication against him in subsequent proceedings, and disqualification for public employment.

Mintz explains: "Based on the idea that young people were less culpable than adults and became delinquent as a result of immaturity, poor parenting, neglect, and poverty, the juvenile courts

FROM THE BENCH

In Re Gault, 387 U.S. 1, 14–16 (1967)

From the inception of the juvenile court system, wide differences have been tolerated, indeed insisted upon, between the procedural rights accorded to adults and those of juveniles. In practically all jurisdictions, there are rights granted to adults which are withheld from juveniles. In addition to the specific problems involved in the present case, for example, it has been held that the juvenile is not entitled to bail, to indictment by grand jury, to a public trial or to trial by jury. It is frequent practice that rules governing the arrest and interrogation of adults by the police are not observed in the case of juveniles.

The history and theory underlying this development are well-known, but a recapitulation is necessary for purposes of this opinion. The Juvenile Court movement began in this country at the end of the last century. From the juvenile court statute adopted in Illinois in 1899, the system has spread to every State in the Union, the District of Columbia, and Puerto Rico. The constitutionality of Juvenile Court laws has been sustained in over 40 jurisdictions against a variety of attacks.

The early reformers were appalled by adult procedures and penalties, and by the fact that children could be given long prison sentences and mixed in jails with hardened criminals. They were profoundly convinced that society's duty to the child could not be confined by the concept of justice alone. They believed that society's role was not to ascertain whether the child was "guilty" or "innocent," but "What is he, how has he become what he is, and what had best be done in his interest and in the interest of the state to save him from a downward career." The child—essentially good, as they saw it—was to be made "to feel that he is the object of [the state's] care and solicitude," not that he was under arrest or on trial. The rules of criminal procedure were therefore altogether inapplicable. The apparent rigidities, technicalities, and harshness which they observed in both substantive and procedural criminal law were therefore to be discarded. The idea of crime and punishment was to be abandoned. The child was to be "treated" and "rehabilitated" and the procedures, from apprehension through institutionalization, were to be "clinical" rather than punitive.

provided wayward youths with the opportunity to turn their lives around."[9] Juvenile courts sprouted up all over the country. By 1925, 46 states had some type of juvenile court.[10] Former New York Supreme Court Justice Irving I. Goldsmith told an audience in Syracuse, New York, in 1933: "The recent development of the children's court reflects the modern attitude of salvaging neglected, destitute and delinquent children, in contrast to the ancient concept of dealing with them through a court of criminal justice."[11]

The problem of juvenile crime never went away, however, and detractors derided the progressive ideas of Tuthill and Lindsey as overly idealistic. Many juvenile reform schools suffered from the problems of runaway children and continued crime. Some of the schools were not run with the passion and true zeal of reformers such as Lindsey.[12]

Lack of Safeguards and U.S. Supreme Court Protections

Other problems included the lack of procedural oversight over juvenile courts themselves and concerns about whether treatment worked for certain groups of juvenile offenders. In the 1960s, the U.S. Supreme Court wanted to ensure that juvenile courts provided at least some protection to young defendants. While juvenile courts were founded on the progressive ideal of treating wayward youths, in practice many operated as institutions without oversight and failed to provide juveniles the legal protections given to adult defendants, including the right to counsel, notice of charges, and failure to notify parent of charges. In *Kent v. United States* (1966), the U.S. Supreme Court decided a case involving whether juvenile defendant Morris Kent, who was accused of robbery and rape, should be transferred to adult criminal court. The Court focused on the lack of procedural protections in determining when a juvenile should be sent to adult court. The Court, in an opinion authored by Justice Abe Fortas, wrote:

Society's attitude toward the prosecution of juveniles as adults has changed in recent decades. In the 1980s and 1990s, about 100 years after the first juvenile courts were established, various state legislatures enacted laws that made it easier to try minors in adult courts, in response to an upsurge in juvenile crime.

We do not consider whether on the merits, Kent should have been transferred; but there is no place in our system of law for reaching a result of such tremendous consequences without ceremony—without hearing, without effective assistance of counsel, without a statement of reasons. It is inconceivable that a court of justice dealing with adults, with respect to a similar issue, would proceed in this manner.[13]

Fortas also noted that "there is much evidence that some juvenile courts . . . lack the personnel, facilities and techniques to perform adequately as representatives of the State in a *parens patriae* capacity, at least with respect to children charged with law violation."[14]

The next year the Court determined in *In Re Gault* (1967) that juvenile court defendants are entitled to a level of due-process protection.[15] The case involved a 15-year-old Arizona youth named Gerald Gault who was sentenced to six years in jail for making an obscene phone call to a neighbor. During the legal proceedings, Gault's parents were not informed of his arrest and he was not given a lawyer or a chance to prove he was innocent. He received a much longer sentence in juvenile court than he would have in adult criminal court.

Fortas proclaimed that "under our Constitution, the condition of being a boy does not justify a kangaroo court."[16] The Court emphasized that the Constitution requires that juveniles have many of the constitutional rights as those charged in adult criminal courts, including the right to counsel, the right to confront witnesses, and the right to notice of criminal charges.

The U.S. Supreme Court later determined in *In Re Winship* (1970) that in juvenile proceedings—often in which the state seeks to prove that a juvenile is delinquent (sometimes called delinquency proceedings)—the prosecution has to prove its case by the difficult standard of beyond a reasonable doubt.[17] This is the same evidentiary standard used in adult criminal law cases.

McKeiver v. Pennsylvania, 403 U.S. 528, 543–546 (1971)

All the litigants here agree that the applicable due process standard in juvenile proceedings, as developed by Gault and Winship, is fundamental fairness. As that standard was applied in those two cases, we have an emphasis on factfinding procedures. The requirements of notice, counsel, confrontation, cross-examination, and standard of proof naturally flowed from this emphasis. But one cannot say that in our legal system the jury is a necessary component of accurate fact-finding. There is much to be said for it, to be sure, but we have been content to pursue other ways for determining facts. Juries are not required, and have not been, for example, in equity cases, in workmen's compensation, in probate, or in deportation cases. Neither have they been generally used in military trials. . . .

Despite all these disappointments, all these failures, and all these shortcomings, we conclude that trial by jury in the juvenile court's adjudicative stage is not a constitutional requirement. We so conclude for a number of reasons:

1. The Court has refrained, in the cases heretofore decided, from taking the easy way with a flat holding that all rights constitutionally assured for the adult accused are to be imposed upon the state juvenile proceeding. What was done in Gault and in Winship is aptly described in *Commonwealth v. Johnson*, 211 Pa.Super. 62, 74, 234 A.2d 9, 15 (1967):

"It is clear to us that the Supreme Court has properly attempted to strike a judicious balance by injecting procedural orderliness into the juvenile court system. It is seeking to reverse the trend (pointed out in Kent, 383 U.S., at 556, 86 S.Ct. 1045) whereby 'the child receives the worst of both worlds. . . .'"

2. There is a possibility, at least, that the jury trial, if required as a matter of constitutional precept, will remake the juvenile proceeding into a fully adversary process and will put an effective end to what has been the idealistic prospect of an intimate, informal protective proceeding.

3. The Task Force Report, although concededly pre-*Gault*, is notable for its not making any recommendation that the jury trial be imposed upon the juvenile court system. This is so despite its vivid description of the system's deficiencies and disappointments. Had the Commission deemed this vital to the integrity of the juvenile process, or to the handling of juveniles, surely a recommendation or suggestion to this effect would have appeared. The intimations, instead, are quite the other way. . . . Further, it expressly recommends against abandonment of the system and against the return of the juvenile to the criminal courts.

The U.S. Supreme Court has made clear, however, that juveniles do not possess the same level of constitutional rights as adults. This becomes clear if one contrasts juvenile delinquency proceedings with adult criminal court cases. The Supreme Court determined in *McKeiver v. Pennsylvania* (1971) that juveniles are not entitled to jury trials under the Constitution as adult defendants are.[18] The Court explained that the basic requirement of fundamental fairness articulated in the *Gault* and *Winship* cases did not demand a jury trial, that the juvenile court judge could ensure that juveniles receive a fair hearing in their courtrooms, and that introducing juries could turn juvenile proceedings into full-fledged adversarial battles like regular adult criminal courtrooms.

A Get-Tough Attitude

The compassionate attitude toward juveniles changed dramatically beginning in the 1970s, and particularly in the mid-1990s, because of an alarming increase in juvenile crime. Much of this was attributed to a fear—often quite reasonable—of juvenile street gangs that wreaked havoc on communities.[19]

As the juvenile crime rate soared, politicians responded by changing juvenile criminal laws. Author John Hubner writes: "A century later [after the creation of the first juvenile court], during the 1980s and 1990s, legislators in state after state were hard at work demolishing the juvenile justice system with wrecking balls, as if the courts were relics of a bygone era."[20] States passed a series of get-tough laws that made it easier for juveniles to be tried as adults. Juvenile transfer laws became the norm, as more juvenile defendants were escorted into criminal court. Many treatment facilities for juveniles did not receive the support they had received in the past.

This book examines several hot-button issues related to the current juvenile justice system. The first major issue deals with juvenile transfers or waivers. The pro and con chapters highlight the tension that has existed since the inception of juvenile courts between treatment and punishment. Some argue that juvenile waivers are used too frequently and that too many juveniles end up processed in the adult criminal system, where they are subject to abuse and are likely to resurface in society after a prison term as hardened criminals. Others counter that juvenile waivers must be used more in order to protect society from dangerous repeat offenders.

The second major issue concerns a topic that sharply divides the U.S. Supreme Court, which has changed position on the subject in the past quarter century: the death penalty for juveniles. In 1989, the Court ruled 5–4 that juvenile murderers could be executed.[21] In 2005, however, the Court reversed that decision, ruling 5–4 that juvenile murderers could not be executed.[22] The Court's deep division in this area provides an excellent discussion point on whether juveniles truly should be treated differently than adults in the legal system. The death penalty chapters examine whether juveniles are more or less likely to be deterred from committing criminal acts by the specter of the death penalty.

The death-penalty issue leads logically to another pressing issue in juvenile justice—whether juveniles should be subject to the sentence of life imprisonment without the possibility of parole. Critics contend that, like the death penalty, a life sentence constitutes "cruel and unusual" punishment under the Eighth Amendment. Others counter that life imprisonment is important in a society that must protect public safety from violent repeat offenders and from juvenile sexual predators.

Juveniles Should Not Be Treated as Adults

When a juvenile defendant is transferred to adult criminal court, the legal system refers to this as a waiver. It means that the juvenile court waives authority over the juvenile and his or her future resides in adult criminal court. There are three basic methods of transferring juveniles: judicial waiver; prosecutorial waiver; and legislative or statutory waiver. In the judicial waiver, a juvenile court judge decides whether to send a juvenile court defendant to adult court. In the prosecutorial waiver, the prosecutor exercises his or her discretion as to whether a juvenile will be charged and processed as an adult or juvenile. Some states have passed laws known as "direct file waiver" laws to give prosecutors such power.[1] Finally, the legislative waiver or exclusion system applies when a law provides that juveniles who commit certain crimes above certain ages must be tried as adults.

Significantly, a juvenile transferred by a prosecutor's decision or by a state law automatically cannot appeal those decisions.

About 200,000 juveniles are sent directly to adult prison each year.[2] Nearly every state has increased the number of waivers over the years by increasing the number of criminal offenses for which juveniles are eligible for transfer or automatically transferred.[3] This is far too many, as juveniles deserve

THE LETTER OF THE LAW

Excerpt from the Kansas Law on Juvenile Transfers, K.S.A. 38-2347

(e) In determining whether or not prosecution as an adult should be authorized or designating the proceeding as an extended jurisdiction juvenile prosecution, the court shall consider each of the following factors:

(1) The seriousness of the alleged offense and whether the protection of the community requires prosecution as an adult or designating the proceeding as an extended jurisdiction juvenile prosecution;

(2) whether the alleged offense was committed in an aggressive, violent, premeditated or willful manner;

(3) whether the offense was against a person or against property. Greater weight shall be given to offenses against persons, especially if personal injury resulted;

(4) the number of alleged offenses unadjudicated and pending against the juvenile;

(5) the previous history of the juvenile, including whether the juvenile had been adjudicated a juvenile offender under this code or the Kansas juvenile justice code and, if so, whether the offenses were against persons or property, and any other previous history of antisocial behavior or patterns of physical violence;

(6) the sophistication or maturity of the juvenile as determined by consideration of the juvenile's home, environment, emotional attitude, pattern of living or desire to be treated as an adult;

(7) whether there are facilities or programs available to the court which are likely to rehabilitate the juvenile prior to the expiration of the court's jurisdiction under this code; and

(8) whether the interests of the juvenile or of the community would be better served by criminal prosecution or extended jurisdiction juvenile prosecution.

the chance for rehabilitation. In stark terms, they are still salvageable.

The push for more transfers is based on misperceptions.

One legal commentator refers to the driving force for more transfers as the "mythical youth violence epidemic."[4] Since 1994,

---

The insufficiency of evidence pertaining to any one or more of the factors listed in this subsection, in and of itself, shall not be determinative of the issue. Subject to the provisions of K.S.A. 38-2354, and amendments thereto, written reports and other materials relating to the juvenile's mental, physical, educational and social history may be considered by the court.

(f)(1) The court may authorize prosecution as an adult upon completion of the hearing if the court finds from a preponderance of the evidence that the alleged juvenile offender should be prosecuted as an adult for the offense charged. In that case, the court shall direct the alleged juvenile offender be prosecuted under the applicable criminal statute and that the proceedings filed under this code be dismissed.

(2) The court may designate the proceeding as an extended jurisdiction juvenile prosecution upon completion of the hearing if the juvenile has failed to rebut the presumption or the court finds from a preponderance of the evidence that the juvenile should be prosecuted under an extended jurisdiction juvenile prosecution.

(3) After a proceeding in which prosecution as an adult is requested pursuant to subsection (a)(2), and prosecution as an adult is not authorized, the court may designate the proceedings to be an extended jurisdiction juvenile prosecution.

(4) A juvenile who is the subject of an extended jurisdiction juvenile prosecution shall have the right to a trial by jury, to the effective assistance of counsel and to all other rights of a defendant pursuant to the Kansas code of criminal procedure. Each court shall adopt local rules to establish the basic procedures for extended jurisdiction juvenile prosecution in such court's jurisdiction.

juvenile crime has gone down, rather than up. When there was great hype about a rise in juvenile crime in the mid-1990s, states passed a series of laws that provided for more juveniles entering the adult criminal system. Juvenile offenders became known as violent super-predators. "Driven by public outrage, crime control advocates adopted a campaign against the juvenile 'super-predator.' "[5] Much of the move to control juvenile "super-predators" comes from excessive media coverage of certain horrific crimes committed by juveniles.[6]

Sending juveniles into adult criminal court only creates more violent offenders.

A 2007 report by the Task Force on Community Preventive Services, which reviewed many studies of juvenile offenders, concluded that transfer policies do not work very well and do not deter future crime. The report found that "transfer policies have generally resulted in increased arrests for subsequent crimes, including violent crime, among teens sent to the adult system, compared to those who remain in juvenile court."[7]

One study examining juveniles in the greater New York City and New Jersey area concluded that juveniles transferred to the adult system were 39 percent more likely to be re-arrested on a violence-related charge than those juveniles who stayed in the juvenile system.[8] Another study done of juveniles arrested on suspicion of felonies in Florida found that "transferred youth had 34% more felony re-arrests than retained youth."[9] Another study of juveniles arrested for felonies in Hennepin County, Minnesota, concluded that those transferred to adult court were 26.5 percent more likely to face further criminal convictions than those retained in the juvenile system.[10] The Task Force on Community Preventive Services concluded that "to the extent that transfer polices are implemented to reduce violent or other criminal behavior, available evidence indicates that they do more harm than good"[11] and that "the review [of the studies] indicates that use of transfer laws and strengthened transfer policies is counterproductive to reducing juvenile violence and enhancing public safety."[12] Judge Greg Mathis, the host of a television court show, notes that many juveniles who transfer to adult prisons return to society even more dangerous. "Many are eventually returned home, lacking the education and skills they need to become productive citizens," Mathis writes. "They return to a life of crime, this time using the knowledge they gained while in prison."[13]

Perhaps even more disturbingly, transfers of juveniles to adult courts often are not used on the most violent offenders.[14] Many times the transfer option is used on nonviolent juveniles.

Sending juveniles to prison leads to more abuse.

There are often tragic consequences of sending juveniles to prison. In some states they are housed in the same facilities as adult prisoners. Other states provide for separate accommodations for juvenile offenders. The reality, however, is that those housed in the adult criminal system are far more likely to be sexually assaulted or face violence. Those juveniles sent to adult prison are also much more likely to commit suicide. Building Blocks for Youths reports: "Research demonstrates that children in adult institutions are five times as likely to be sexually assaulted, twice as likely to be beaten by staff, 50 percent more likely to be attacked with a weapon, and eight times as likely to commit suicide as children confined in juvenile facilities."[15]

This abuse can occur even in those states or places where juveniles are housed with other young people in a penal institution. Kelly M. Angell writes: "Even juveniles who remain housed with other juveniles can suffer permanent and debilitating harm just by virtue of being incarcerated."[16]

Transferring juveniles does not deter future crime.

Transferring more juveniles to adult courts also does not deter other juveniles from committing crimes. A theory behind using

In May 2005, Seung Hong, the communications director of Juvenile Justice Project of Louisiana, talks with Dwight Gilbert and his mother, Kimberly Johnson, in his office in New Orleans. When Johnson went to visit her teenage son during the two years he was in the East Baton Rouge Parish lockup, she often found him injured from fighting with his fellow inmates. The state has sought to reform its youth correctional system, which has seen reports of violence and abuse rising in recent years.

more waivers or transfers is that transferring some juvenile offenders will send a clear message to their friends and/or associates and thereby serve as a general deterrent. In other words, the theory is that transferring some juvenile offenders will deter other juveniles from committing similar crimes.

The evidence, however, does not support this deterrence theory. Two professors who conducted a general study of the effect of direct file waiver laws concluded: "We feel confident in inferring from our results that direct file laws have had little effect on violent juvenile crime."[17] The authors point out that previous studies and the U.S. Supreme Court in *Roper v. Simmons* (2005) indicated that juveniles were not deterred by the imposition of the death penalty and note:

> Thus, if juveniles are unlikely to be deterred by the potential of receiving a death sentence when committing the most serious of illegal acts, it seems improbable that the possibility that they could be transferred to criminal court for committing a similar, although typically less severe, crime would weigh heavily on their decision-making process.[18]

Juveniles are less able to understand the adult criminal process.

Placing juveniles into the adult criminal system puts them at greater risk in part because they do not understand the criminal system as well as adults. Many juveniles are unfamiliar with such legal concepts as waiver of rights or Miranda rights, and are more vulnerable to enduring manipulative police interrogations without an attorney present. Juveniles give coerced confessions more often than adults do because they do not understand their rights. More juveniles waive their right to the assistance of legal counsel (an attorney) because they do not fully appreciate the need for an attorney in a criminal case. Two legal commentators argue that juvenile courts are "a breeding ground for wrongful convictions."[19] "Even youths who understand the abstract words of a Miranda warning or judicial advisory of counsel may not be able to exercise their rights effectively," writes law professor Barry Feld. "Juveniles may not appreciate the function or importance of rights as well as do adults."[20]

Adult criminal records are damaging to juveniles' futures.

One reason that more juveniles should not be hauled into adult criminal court concerns their future in life. Convictions

---

FROM THE BENCH

Miranda v. Arizona, 384 U.S. 436, 444–445 (1966)

In *Miranda v. Arizona*, the U.S. Supreme Court invalidated the coerced confession of defendant Ernesto Miranda, who was interrogated for multiple hours without being informed of his legal rights. In its decision, the Court established that suspects in police custody and those arrested have the right to be informed of their rights. These are called Miranda rights. The Court explained in this excerpt:

> Our holding will be spelled out with some specificity in the pages which follow but briefly stated it is this: the prosecution may not use statements, whether exculpatory or inculpatory, stemming from custodial interrogation of the defendant unless it demonstrates the use of procedural safeguards effective to secure the privilege against self-incrimination. By custodial interrogation, we mean questioning initiated by law enforcement officers after a person has been taken into custody or otherwise deprived of his freedom of action in any significant way. As for the procedural safeguards to be employed, unless other fully effective means are devised to inform accused persons of their right of silence and to assure a continuous opportunity to exercise it, the following measures are required. Prior to any questioning, the person must be warned that he has a right to remain silent, that any statement he does make may be used as evidence against him, and that he has a right to the presence of an attorney, either retained or appointed. The defendant may waive effectuation of these rights, provided the waiver is made voluntarily, knowingly and intelligently. If, however, he indicates in any manner and at any stage of the process that he wishes to consult with an attorney before speaking there can be no questioning. Likewise, if the individual is alone and indicates in any manner that he does not wish to be interrogated, the police may not question him. The mere fact that he may have answered some questions or volunteered some statements on his own does not deprive him of the right to refrain from answering any further inquiries until he has consulted with an attorney and thereafter consents to be questioned.

in juvenile court normally are sealed (meaning they are not publicly known), while convictions in adult criminal court are a matter of public record. This means that a conviction in adult criminal court can diminish opportunities and brand people as dangerous and untrustworthy. One legal commentator explains that "incarcerating children in adult prisons has devastating effects on the juvenile offenders well beyond the realm of just punishment."[21] Furthermore, "the more difficult it is for a juvenile to find a stable job, the more likely he will recidivate," meaning commit another crime.[22] Most juveniles deserve better treatment.

Summary

Increasing numbers of juveniles are transferred into adult criminal courts. This has occurred because of hype and misconception about allegedly increasing juvenile crime. Sending more juveniles to prison leads to more violent offenders down the road and subjects juveniles to a greater risk of physical abuse. Transferring more juveniles to adult court does not deter juvenile crime in general and in fact places them in potential peril from a legal standpoint, as they are not able to understand their legal rights and protections as well as adults. Perhaps even more significantly, being placed in the adult criminal system with its permanent recordings of crimes stigmatizes individuals and has real-world ramifications long after the person is released into society.

The American justice system must find ways to rehabilitate juvenile offenders rather than simply send them "up the river" to adult prisons. As Judge Mathis writes: "We cannot incarcerate our way out of society's ills."[23]

Some Juveniles Should Be Treated as Adults

A terrifying and horrific crime spree, which included the deaths of two students at two prestigious universities, could have been prevented if the juvenile system had acted appropriately. According to police reports, on January 18, 2008, 17-year-old Lawrence Alvin Lovette Jr. allegedly killed Duke graduate student Abhijit Mahato. A little more than a week later, on January 29, Lovette allegedly stole a car and committed a burglary, then committed a robbery in February. Later in March, he allegedly killed Eve Carson, president of the student body at the University of North Carolina at Chapel Hill. Lovette had committed numerous crimes as a minor, earning time in juvenile prison. The system treated him too leniently, however, and he was paroled after only 14 months. He committed another serious crime as a juvenile and received only a slap on the wrist. On January 16, 2008, Lovette pleaded guilty to three misdemeanor crimes and received only probation. Two days later Mahato was slain.[1]

The problem, as one official said, is that "you have a long juvenile record and go to adult court and be a virgin defendant."[2] The system is too lenient for violent juveniles who are repeat offenders. These defendants need to be tried in adult court, because public safety should be the paramount concern of the legal system. It is noble to try to rehabilitate a juvenile, but that ideal should not obscure the harsh reality that there are certain juvenile predators who must be incarcerated for long periods of time. Otherwise, more people will meet the same fate that Abhijit Mahato and Eve Carson did.

There are different types of waivers.

There are various ways in which a juvenile comes into contact with the adult criminal system. A juvenile court judge can transfer a juvenile to criminal court, finding that the specific individual is not receptive to further treatment options. This is called a judicial waiver. Prosecutorial waiver occurs when a district attorney decides to prosecute a juvenile as an adult. This form is often referred to as concurrent jurisdiction.[3] Another type of waiver is a statutory or legislative waiver. This occurs when a state law provides that certain crimes committed by juveniles above a certain age must be tried in adult criminal court.[4]

All 50 states have some mechanism for trying juveniles as adults in criminal courts. In some states, a waiver to send the accused to adult court takes place if a juvenile above a certain age commits a violent felony. Other states provide for a series of factors that the juvenile court or the prosecutor can consider.[5] The states differ as to the minimum age at which a juvenile can be transferred. They also differ in the factors that are to be considered before transferring a juvenile to adult court. Many states consider the severity of the crime, the criminal history of the juvenile, and whether efforts at treatment have been successful.

Waiver Provisions for Trying Juveniles as Adults

The following is an excerpt from a document written by the Office of Juvenile Justice and Delinquency Prevention detailing the different kinds of waiver provisions:

> All States have provisions for trying certain juveniles as adults in criminal court. This is known as *transfer to criminal court*. There are three basic transfer mechanisms: *judicial waiver*, *statutory exclusion*, and *concurrent jurisdiction*.

> Under judicial waiver provisions the juvenile court judge has the authority to waive juvenile court jurisdiction and transfer the case to criminal court.

> Waiver provisions vary in terms of the degree of flexibility allowed. Some waiver provisions are entirely *discretionary*. In other provisions there is a rebuttable *presumption* in favor of waiver, and in others waiver is *mandatory* once the juvenile court judge determines that certain statutory criteria have been met.

> As of the end of the 2004 legislative session, 45 states and the District of Columbia allow juvenile court judges to waive jurisdiction over certain cases and transfer them to criminal court, a practice known as judicial waiver.

> Age and offense criteria are common components of judicial waiver provisions, but other factors come into play as well. For example, most state statutes limit judicial waiver to juveniles who are "no longer amenable to treatment." The specific factors that determine lack of amenability vary, but they typically include the juvenile's offending history and previous dispositional outcomes.

> Many (18) states with judicial waiver provisions establish 14 as the minimum age for waiver, but there is variation across states. The provisions in Kansas and Vermont, for example, permit 10-year-olds to be waived.

Source: Office of Juvenile Justice and Delinquency Prevention, http://ojjdp.ncjrs.gov/ojstatbb/structure_process/qa04110.asp.

For example, Indiana's law requires that the juvenile offender be at least 14 years of age, have committed an "aggravated" felony, and be "beyond rehabilitation under the juvenile justice system."[6] Oregon's law requires that the juvenile be at least 15 and have committed a violent felony, and considers "the amenability of the youth to treatment and rehabilitation given the techniques, facilities and personnel for rehabilitation available to the juvenile court and to the criminal court which would have jurisdiction after transfer."[7]

Blended sentencing provides a better option than just juvenile court sentences.

One approach that perhaps serves the best of both worlds is a phenomenon known as blended sentencing. Blended sentencing combines the authority of both juvenile and adult criminal courts. Sometimes these laws are called extended juvenile jurisdiction laws. Juvenile blended sentencing schemes give juvenile court judges the power to sentence a juvenile to a traditional juvenile-type sentence (often to a treatment center or boot camp), but if the juvenile fails the program, the judge has the option of sending the juvenile into criminal court. At least 26 states have some form of blended sentencing for juveniles.[8] These systems are known as juvenile blended sentencing schemes or criminal blended sentencing schemes. In a juvenile blending sentencing scheme, the juvenile court can impose adult criminal sanctions on a youth. In a criminal blended sentencing scheme, adult criminal courts can impose sentences more often given in juvenile court.[9] The common element of blended sentencing schemes is they "allow the judge a choice of which type of sentence he or she wishes to impose, i.e. either juvenile or adult."[10]

Texas, for example, has a determinate type of blending sentencing in which juveniles often determine the outcome of their

(continues on page 36)

THE LETTER OF THE LAW

Excerpts from Juvenile State Waiver Laws

Indiana's Juvenile Waiver Law

31-30-3-2. Heinous or aggravated acts—Patterns of delinquent acts.

Upon motion of the prosecuting attorney and after full investigation and hearing, the juvenile court may waive jurisdiction if it finds that:

   (1) the child is charged with an act that is a felony:

      (A) that is heinous or aggravated, with greater weight given to acts against the person than to acts against property; or

      (B) that is a part of a repetitive pattern of delinquent acts, even though less serious;

   (2) the child was at least fourteen (14) years of age when the act charged was allegedly committed;

   (3) there is probable cause to believe that the child committed the act;

   (4) the child is beyond rehabilitation under the juvenile justice system; and

   (5) it is in the best interests of the safety and welfare of the community that the child stand trial as an adult.*

Michigan's Judicial Waiver Law

§ 712A.4. Waiver of jurisdiction when child of 14 or older accused of felony.

   (1) If a juvenile 14 years of age or older is accused of an act that if committed by an adult would be a felony, the judge of the family division of circuit court in the county in which the offense is alleged to have been committed may waive jurisdiction under this section upon motion of the prosecuting attorney. After waiver, the juvenile may be tried in the court having general criminal jurisdiction of the offense.

   (2) Before conducting a hearing on the motion to waive jurisdiction, the court shall give notice of the hearing in the manner provided by supreme court rule to the juvenile and the prosecuting attorney and, if addresses are known, to the juvenile's parents or guardians. The notice shall state clearly that a waiver of jurisdiction to a court of general criminal jurisdiction has been requested and that, if granted, the juvenile can be prosecuted for the alleged offense as though he or she were an adult.

   (3) Before the court waives jurisdiction, the court shall determine on the record if there is probable cause to believe that an offense has been committed that if committed by an adult would be a felony and if there is probable

cause to believe that the juvenile committed the offense. Before a juvenile may waive a probable cause hearing under this subsection, the court shall inform the juvenile that a waiver of this subsection waives the preliminary examination required by . . . the code of criminal procedure. . . .

(4) Upon a showing of probable cause under subsection (3), the court shall conduct a hearing to determine if the best interests of the juvenile and the public would be served by granting a waiver of jurisdiction to the court of general criminal jurisdiction. In making its determination, the court shall consider all of the following criteria, giving greater weight to the seriousness of the alleged offense and the juvenile's prior record of delinquency than to the other criteria:

(a) The seriousness of the alleged offense in terms of community protection, including, but not limited to, the existence of any aggravating factors recognized by the sentencing guidelines, the use of a firearm or other dangerous weapon, and the impact on any victim.

(b) The culpability of the juvenile in committing the alleged offense, including, but not limited to, the level of the juvenile's participation in planning and carrying out the offense and the existence of any aggravating or mitigating factors recognized by the sentencing guidelines.

(c) The juvenile's prior record of delinquency including, but not limited to, any record of detention, any police record, any school record, or any other evidence indicating prior delinquent behavior.

(d) The juvenile's programming history, including, but not limited to, the juvenile's past willingness to participate meaningfully in available programming.

(e) The adequacy of the punishment or programming available in the juvenile justice system.

(f) The dispositional options available for the juvenile.

(5) If the court determines that there is probable cause to believe that an offense has been committed that if committed by an adult would be a felony and that the juvenile committed the offense, the court shall waive jurisdiction of the juvenile if the court finds that the juvenile has previously been subject to the jurisdiction of the circuit court. . . .

(8) The court shall enter a written order either granting or denying the motion to waive jurisdiction and the court shall state on the record or in a written

(continues)

THE LETTER OF THE LAW

(continued)

opinion the court's findings of fact and conclusions of law forming the basis for entering the order. If a juvenile is waived, a transcript of the court's findings or a copy of the written opinion shall be sent to the court of general criminal jurisdiction. . . .

(11) As used in this section, "felony" means an offense punishable by imprisonment for more than 1 year or an offense designated by law as a felony.**

* Burns Ind. Code Ann. § 31-30-3-2 (2009).
**MCLS § 712A.4.

(continued from page 33)

sentencing by their behavior.[11] If a youth completes a program at a treatment-type facility, then the counselors and officials at the program will recommend that the juvenile receive parole. If the youth does not complete the program to the satisfaction of the officials, then the youth is transferred to an adult facility and will serve a longer portion of his or her original sentence.[12]

Blended sentencing offers the options of treatment and punishment for juveniles. If the juvenile appears receptive to treatment, he or she can rehabilitate and perhaps integrate back into society successfully. If the juvenile offender does not adhere or accept treatment, then the juvenile can be punished with a more traditional criminal sentence and the public is protected.

Transferring some juveniles to adult criminal court protects society.

Common sense explains why certain juveniles are transferred to adult criminal court. These juveniles are repeat offenders whose rap sheets often demonstrate escalating violence. Transferring these offenders to adult criminal court increases the punishments most of the time and takes these offenders off the streets, where they could commit more crimes. "Since the cost to society is the same regardless of the age of the criminal, why should repeat juvenile offenders receive lighter sentences than adults?" asks Robert Sexton. "After all it is no secret that juvenile courts are considerably more lenient than adult courts."[13]

Gangs have capitalized on the more lenient sentences generally given to juveniles. San Mateo County, California, District Attorney James Fox explained to Congress: "Because many states mandate lesser penalties for violent juvenile offenders than adults, gang leadership often have juvenile gang members perform violent crimes towards others because there is less of an ability to prosecute them."[14]

Waivers are particularly necessary for a breed of juveniles who continually re-offend and have rap sheets that are extremely long. These continuing patterns of criminal activity make it increasingly unlikely that treatment will ever work. "It is also a well-known fact that most juvenile crime is committed by 'chronic offenders.'"[15] Transferring these juveniles to adult criminal court also helps because there is greater access to criminal records in adult court. There are no barriers to finding past crimes and criminal history, as there are sometimes in finding out juvenile records.

The public supports waivers of juvenile offenders to adult courts.

In a democracy, the will of the people most often should prevail. Public opinion polls routinely show that a sizeable majority of Americans favor transferring violent juveniles to adult criminal court.[16] Another poll found that 83 percent of those surveyed wanted juveniles and adults treated the same with respect to violent crime.[17] A Gallup poll conducted in November 2003 found that 59 percent of those surveyed believed that juveniles who commit violent crimes should be tried in adult criminal court.[18]

(continues on page 40)

THE LETTER OF THE LAW

Excerpts from Illinois's Blended Sentencing Law for Juveniles

§ 5-810. Extended jurisdiction juvenile prosecutions.

(1) (a) If the State's Attorney files a petition, at any time prior to commencement of the minor's trial, to designate the proceeding as an extended jurisdiction juvenile prosecution and the petition alleges the commission by a minor 13 years of age or older of any offense which would be a felony if committed by an adult, and, if the juvenile judge assigned to hear and determine petitions to designate the proceeding as an extended jurisdiction juvenile prosecution determines that there is probable cause to believe that the allegations in the petition and motion are true, there is a rebuttable presumption that the proceeding shall be designated as an extended jurisdiction juvenile proceeding.

(b) The judge shall enter an order designating the proceeding as an extended jurisdiction juvenile proceeding unless the judge makes a finding based on clear and convincing evidence that sentencing under the Chapter V of the Unified Code of Corrections would not be appropriate for the minor based on an evaluation of the following factors:

(i) the age of the minor;

(ii) the history of the minor, including:

(A) any previous delinquent or criminal history of the minor,

(B) any previous abuse or neglect history of the minor, and

(C) any mental health, physical and/or educational history of the minor;

(iii) the circumstances of the offense, including:

(A) the seriousness of the offense,

(B) whether the minor is charged through accountability,

(C) whether there is evidence the offense was committed in an aggressive and premeditated manner,

(D) whether there is evidence the offense caused serious bodily harm,

(E) whether there is evidence the minor possessed a deadly weapon;

      (iv) the advantages of treatment within the juvenile justice system including whether there are facilities or programs, or both, particularly available in the juvenile system;

      (v) whether the security of the public requires sentencing under Chapter V of the Unified Code of Corrections:

        (A) the minor's history of services, including the minor's willingness to participate meaningfully in available services;

        (B) whether there is a reasonable likelihood that the minor can be rehabilitated before the expiration of the juvenile court's jurisdiction;

        (C) the adequacy of the punishment or services.

In considering these factors, the court shall give greater weight to the seriousness of the alleged offense and the minor's prior record of delinquency than to other factors listed in this subsection. . . .

(4) Sentencing. If an extended jurisdiction juvenile prosecution under subsection (1) results in a guilty plea, a verdict of guilty, or a finding of guilt, the court shall impose the following:

    (i) one or more juvenile sentences . . . ; and

    (ii) an adult criminal sentence . . .

(6) When it appears that a minor convicted in an extended jurisdiction juvenile prosecution under subsection (1) has violated the conditions of his or her sentence, or is alleged to have committed a new offense upon the filing of a petition to revoke the stay, the court may, without notice, issue a warrant for the arrest of the minor. After a hearing, if the court finds by a preponderance of the evidence that the minor committed a new offense, the court shall order execution of the previously imposed adult criminal sentence. . . .

(7) Upon successful completion of the juvenile sentence the court shall vacate the adult criminal sentence.

Source: 705 ILCS 405/5-810.

(continued from page 37)

Summary

Juvenile crime remains a serious problem in American society. Too many chronic or repeat juvenile offenders continue to commit criminal offenses and receive lax sentences. This does not protect the public. For this reason, states should increase the waiver or transfer option for juveniles who commit violent felonies or those who re-offend. The public's safety must be the top priority in the legal system. Blended sentencing is an option that many states have adopted because it keeps open both the treatment and punishment options available in the juvenile and adult criminal systems. On this matter, our lawmakers and judges should also keep in mind the will of the majority of Americans, who support measures to protect the innocent from violent, repeat juvenile offenders.

Juveniles Should Not Receive the Death Penalty

Thirteen-year-old Brenton Butler was walking to a Block-buster video store when he was picked up for murder in Jacksonville, Florida. Police interrogated him for 12 hours before finally eliciting a confession under the most coercive of circumstances. Although a jury eventually found Butler not guilty, he spent six months behind bars awaiting trial.[1]

An even worse miscarriage of justice happened to then-14-year-old Calvin Ollins, a mentally disabled boy who was charged, along with his cousin Larry and two other teens, in the killing of a young medical student. In 1988, a jury convicted Ollins, then 15, of murder, aggravated sexual assault, and aggravated kidnapping.[2] Ollins' aunt told the *Chicago Tribune* after her nephew's conviction: "They didn't have no fingerprints, no blood, no nothing. All they had was a false confession forced on a retarded child."[3]

It turned out that Ollins' aunt—not the police or the prosecutors—was correct. Her nephew did not murder the medical student. In December 2001, Calvin Ollins and the other convicted teens were released from prison after DNA tests conclusively proved they did not commit these awful crimes. Ollins said that prosecutors "tried to kill me. They tried to put me under the rug and just forget about me."[4] Illinois's then-governor, George Ryan, later pardoned Ollins. In 2003, Ollins received a settlement for $1.5 million.[5] In 2004, two other men pleaded guilty to the charges and received 75-year sentences.[6]

It was awful for teenager Brenton Butler to spend more than six months in jail and face murder charges for a crime he did not commit. It was even worse for teenager Calvin Ollins to be convicted of murder for a crime he did not commit and spend 13 years in prison. What would be far worse than both these egregious realities would be for a juvenile to be executed for a murder he or she did not commit. These sobering stories should give serious pause to anyone who supports the death penalty for juveniles.

The death penalty is controversial, even for adults.

"Death is different," the U.S. Supreme Court wrote in 1976.[7] It is different because it constitutes the ultimate punishment: the taking of a human life. For this reason, the death penalty remains one of the most divisive and controversial issues facing the United States today. In a 1972 decision, *Furman v. Georgia*, the U.S. Supreme Court invalidated the death penalty, reasoning that it constituted a violation of the Eighth Amendment of the U.S. Constitution: "Excessive bail shall not be required, nor excessive fines imposed, nor cruel and unusual punishments inflicted."[8]

The Court reasoned that death penalty laws in Georgia and other states did not provide sufficient guidance in determining which criminal defendants should receive the death penalty. Justice Potter Stewart, in his concurring opinion, wrote that "these death sentences are cruel and unusual in the same way that being struck by lighting is cruel and unusual."[9] After this decision, no executions took place in the United States until 1977—a year after the U.S. Supreme Court upheld more narrowly crafted death-penalty laws in 1976. A bare majority of the Court in *Gregg v. Georgia* reasoned that these newer state death penalty laws gave sufficient guidance to jurors on when death was a viable sentence.

Although the U.S. Supreme Court reinstated the death penalty, the Court has in more recent years prohibited the death penalty to be imposed on certain categories of defendants. In 1986, the Court ruled in *Ford v. Wainwright* that it would violate the Eighth Amendment to execute persons judged to be insane.[10] In 2002, the Court ruled in *Atkins v. Virginia* that it would violate the Eighth Amendment to execute murderers who are mentally retarded.[11]

In the late 1980s, the Supreme Court struggled with the issue of the death penalty for juveniles, issuing two rulings that almost seemed to contradict each other. In *Thompson v. Oklahoma* (1988), the Court ruled that a state could not execute a juvenile who committed murder when he or she was 15 years of age or younger.[12] The very next year, however, the Court ruled in *Stanford v. Kentucky* (1989) that a state could executive a juvenile murderer who was 16 or 17 at the time of the crime.[13]

In all of these death penalty decisions, the Court asked whether executing these types of defendants comported with "evolving standards of decency."[14] The Court originally used this standard from a nondeath penalty case involving a military deserter. Specifically, the Court wrote that the Eighth Amendment "must draw its meaning from the evolving standards of decency that mark the progress of a maturing society."[15] Evolving standards of decency require at least some recognition from the international community, even if the American judicial system does not specifically use international law in the legal process. The International Covenant on Civil and Political

Rights prohibits executions of juveniles, as does the American Convention on Human Rights.[16]

Juveniles are treated differently under the law, and the death penalty is no exception.

Juveniles cannot vote, serve in the military, or consume alcohol legally. They are treated differently in contract law and family law. Laws in every state emphasize these differences. Why, then, should juveniles who commit murder be treated the same as adult murderers? The easy answer is that they should not be. Juveniles are fundamentally different than adults and, therefore, should be treated differently under most circumstances.

Even in ancient Rome, juveniles received lighter sentences than adults for the identical crime.[17] When talking of the ultimate punishment in society—death at the hand of the state—capital punishment for juveniles is simply a gross and vicious

THE LETTER OF THE LAW

Although the U.S. Supreme Court has upheld the death penalty, its use has been narrowed in recent years, conforming in part to international prohibitions against capital punishment. Excerpts from such international prohibitions are listed below:

International Covenant on Civil and Political Rights, Article 6, No. 5
Sentence of death shall not be imposed for crimes committed by persons below eighteen years of age and shall not be carried out on pregnant women.*

American Convention on Human Rights, Article 4, No. 5
Capital punishment shall not be imposed upon persons who, at the time the crime was committed, were under 18 years of age or over 70 years of age; nor shall it be applied to pregnant women.**

* International Covenant on Civil and Political Rights, http://www2.ohchr.org/english/law/ccpr.htm.
**American Convention on Human Rights, http://www.oas.org/juridico/English/treaties/b-32.html.

overreaction. On March 1, 2005, the U.S. Supreme Court recognized that juvenile murderers are different than adult murderers. The Court ruled in *Roper v. Simmons* (2005) that juveniles could not be executed for the crime of murder (or any other crime).[18] The case involved Shawn Simmons, who committed a murder when he was 17 years old. Under previous Supreme Court case law, notably the Court's 1989 decision in *Stanford v. Kentucky*, juveniles who were 16 and 17 years old could be executed.[19] Since that decision, however, several states had done away with the death penalty for juveniles, and the composition of the Supreme Court had changed. Moreover, world opinion on the death penalty for juveniles had also changed.

In *Roper v. Simmons*, the Court—in an opinion written by Justice Anthony Kennedy—emphasized serious differences between a typical juvenile and a typical adult. Juveniles are more likely to act in an immature, hasty, or reckless manner. Because they have not fully formed their own personalities, juveniles are also more susceptible to the damaging effects of peer pressure.[20] Kennedy also noted that there is a greater chance that a juvenile criminal offender (even a juvenile murderer) could be rehabilitated: "From a moral standpoint it would be misguided to equate the failings of a minor with those of an adult, for a greater possibility exists that a minor's character deficiencies will be reformed."[21]

In this same case, the Court also recognized that the United States differed from virtually every other nation in the world by allowing the execution of juveniles. Kennedy wrote that "our determination that the death penalty is disproportionate punishment for offenders under 18 finds confirmation in the stark reality that the United States is the only country in the world that continues to give official sanction to the juvenile death penalty."[22]

This movement away from the death penalty for juveniles by various states and by foreign countries helped the Court's

FROM THE BENCH

Roper v. Simmons, 543 U.S. 551, 569–570 (2005)

Three general differences between juveniles under 18 and adults demonstrate that juvenile offenders cannot with reliability be classified among the worst offenders. First, as any parent knows and as the scientific and sociological studies respondent and his amici cite tend to confirm, "[a] lack of maturity and an under-developed sense of responsibility are found in youth more often than in adults and are more understandable among the young. These qualities often result in impetuous and ill-considered actions and decisions." . . . It has been noted that "adolescents are overrepresented statistically in virtually every category of reck-less behavior." . . . In recognition of the comparative immaturity and irresponsibil-ity of juveniles, almost every State prohibits those under 18 years of age from voting, serving on juries, or marrying without parental consent.

The second area of difference is that juveniles are more vulnerable or suscep-tible to negative influences and outside pressures, including peer pressure. . . . It is a time and condition of life when a person may be most susceptible to influence and to psychological damage). This is explained in part by the prevailing circum-stance that juveniles have less control, or less experience with control, over their own environment. . . . The third broad difference is that the character of a juvenile is not as well formed as that of an adult. The personality traits of juveniles are more transitory, less fixed. . . .

These differences render suspect any conclusion that a juvenile falls among the worst offenders. The susceptibility of juveniles to immature and irresponsi-ble behavior means "their irresponsible conduct is not as morally reprehensible as that of an adult." Their own vulnerability and comparative lack of control over their immediate surroundings mean juveniles have a greater claim than adults to be forgiven for failing to escape negative influences in their whole environ-ment. The reality that juveniles still struggle to define their identity means it is less supportable to conclude that even a heinous crime committed by a juvenile is evidence of irretrievably depraved character. From a moral stand-point it would be misguided to equate the failings of a minor with those of an adult, for a greater possibility exists that a minor's character deficiencies will be reformed. . . .

Once the diminished culpability of juveniles is recognized, it is evident that the penological justifications for the death penalty apply to them with lesser force than to adults.

majority to rule the way that it did in accordance with the "evolving standards of decency" of the Eighth Amendment.

Serious differences exist between juvenile and adult murderers.

Medical evidence and literature establishes that juveniles do not appreciate the gravity of their actions as much as adults. The Coalition for Juvenile Justice, in its friend-of-the-court brief in *Roper v. Simmons* (2005), related the findings of several studies that clearly showed that juveniles' cognitive development is not as advanced and that juveniles suffer from "developmental deficiencies."[23] Because of these deficiencies, the Coalition noted, juveniles may not be able to provide as much assistance to their legal counsels and may be more likely to incriminate themselves. This is important because it means that juveniles may, unwittingly or unknowingly, compromise their Sixth Amendment right to counsel and their Fifth Amendment protection from self-incrimination.[24]

The American Bar Association persuasively argued before the Supreme Court in its friend-of-the-court brief that juveniles

QUOTABLE

U.S. Supreme Court Associate Justice Anthony Kennedy

Respondent and his amici have submitted, and petitioner does not contest, that only seven countries other than the United States have executed juvenile offenders since 1990: Iran, Pakistan, Saudi Arabia, Yemen, Nigeria, the Democratic Republic of Congo, and China. Since then each of these countries has either abolished capital punishment for juveniles or made public disavowal of the practice. In sum, it is fair to say that the United States now stands alone in a world that has turned its face against the juvenile death penalty.

Source: *Roper v. Simmons*, 543 U.S. 551, 577 (2005).

are "more susceptible to coercion and more likely to be intimidated into making false confessions than are adults."[25] The ABA pointed to the infamous 1989 Central Park jogger case in which a young woman was brutally beaten and raped in Central Park in New York City. Several juveniles confessed to beating and raping the young woman. After these juveniles had served most of their jail sentences, it was discovered that they were not the perpetrators. The danger that this could happen in a death penalty case is simply too great to ignore.[26]

Summary

Juveniles should never face the death penalty, for numerous reasons. They are less mature, less emotionally prepared for the stresses of life, and more likely to be able to rehabilitate themselves if given a second chance. Scientific evidence shows that their cognitive development is simply not the same as adults. Finally, and perhaps most importantly, it is "cruel and unusual" to executive juveniles, particularly when no other country in the world sanctions such a barbaric practice.

Some Older Juveniles Should Receive the Death Penalty

Christopher Simmons, a 17-year-old, told his friends that he wanted to kill someone. He planned to burglarize a house and murder its occupants. He bragged that he and his friends could "get away with it" because they were minors.[1] Simmons and a 15-year-old broke into the house of Mrs. Crook, forced her from her bed, bound and gagged her, and then drove her to a river. They hog-tied her with electrical cable and pushed her into the river, where she drowned.[2] U.S. Supreme Court Justice Sandra Day O'Connor wrote in her dissenting opinion in *Roper v. Simmons* (2005): "One can scarcely imagine the terror that this woman must have suffered throughout the ordeal leading to her death."[3]

In *Roper v. Simmons,* a bare majority of the U.S. Supreme Court (5–4) ruled that a state such as Missouri, where Simmons committed his heinous murder, can never execute minors for murder. This bare majority ruled that executing a juvenile murderer would violate the Eighth Amendment of the U.S. Constitution, which forbids "cruel and unusual punishment." In reaching its decision, the Court overruled one of its prior decisions and impermissibly substituted its own moral judgment instead of a dispassionate legal analysis. The reality is that these five justices overrode the laws of the 20 state legislatures that allowed the execution of juvenile murderers because the justices based their decision in part on international law and their own moral judgment rather than U.S. law.

The Supreme Court in *Roper v. Simmons* wrongly overruled prior law.

A most surprising aspect of the U.S. Supreme Court's decision to invalidate the death sentence of Christopher Simmons was the fact that the Court overruled one of its earlier decisions in order to do so. In *Stanford v. Kentucky* (1989), the Court had ruled that it did not constitute cruel and unusual punishment for the state of Kentucky to execute 17-year-old murderer Kevin N. Stanford. In that case, Stanford and an accomplice robbed a gas station, raped and sodomized the store attendant, drove her to a secluded area of the woods, and shot her in the back of the head.[4] The Court consolidated (combined together) that case with *Wilkins v. Missouri*, a case in which 16-year-old Heath Wilkins stabbed to death a 26-year-old convenience store worker. Wilkins stabbed her to death, according to the record in the case, because "a dead person can't talk."[5]

The Court in *Stanford v. Kentucky* reasoned that many states allowed the execution of those under 18; therefore, there was not a national consensus against executing juvenile murderers. Justice Antonin Scalia noted that of the 37 states that allowed for the death penalty, more than half allowed for the execution of those who killed when they were 16 or 17.[6] Very few states had changed positions between 1989, when the Court decided

States that execute juvenile offenders

Since 1976, 17 U.S. inmates have been executed for crimes committed when they were under age 18. Seventy-three juvenile offenders are on death row in 15 of 23 states that allow juvenile executions.

- 0 Juveniles executed
- 0 Juveniles on death row

Minimum execution age: ■ 16 □ 17

Countries that have executed juvenile offenders since 1990: Congo, Iran, Nigeria, Pakistan, Saudi Arabia, U.S., Yemen

© 2001 KRT
Source: Death Penalty Information Center (U.S.), Amnesty International, Human Rights Watch
Graphic: Chicago Tribune

N.H. 0 0
Idaho 0 0
S.D. 0 0
Pa. 0 3
Del. 0 0
Nev. 0 2
Utah 0 0
Colo. 0 0
Ind. 0 0
Mo. 1 2
Ky. 0 2
Va. 3 1
N.C. 0 1
Ariz. 0 4
Okla. 1 1
Ark. 0 0
S.C. 1 3
Ala. 0 14
Ga. 1 3
Texas 9 26
La. 1 3
Miss. 0 5
Fla. 0 3

This map shows the states that allowed execution of juveniles, the number on death row, and the number executed since 1976, as of 2001. The U.S. Supreme Court prohibited the execution of juveniles in *Roper v. Simmons* in 2005.

Stanford v. Kentucky, and 2005 when the Court decided *Roper v. Simmons*. The only change, therefore, was the one on the Supreme Court itself.

Many juveniles know killing is wrong.

Many older juveniles know that killing is wrong and that they should not do it. Christopher Simmons himself knew what he did was wrong and knew enough to know that he might get away with it because he was a minor. The Justice for All Alliance, which supported the state of Missouri in the Simmons case, pointed out in its friend-of-the-court brief that "age does not define one's character, judgment, maturity, personal responsibility or moral guilt."[7] Justice O'Connor noted: "And Simmons' prediction that he could murder with impunity because he had not yet turned 18—though inaccurate—suggests that he did take into account the perceived risk of punishment in deciding whether to commit the crime."[8]

FROM THE BENCH

Stanford v. Kentucky, 492 U.S. 361, 377–378 (1989)

Having failed to establish a consensus against capital punishment for 16- and 17-year-old offenders through state and federal statutes and the behavior of prosecutors and juries, petitioners seek to demonstrate it through other indicia, including public opinion polls, the views of interest groups, and the positions adopted by various professional associations. We decline the invitation to rest constitutional law upon such uncertain foundations. A revised national consensus so broad, so clear, and so enduring as to justify a permanent prohibition upon all units of democratic government must appear in the operative acts (laws and the application of laws) that the people have approved.

We also reject petitioners' argument that we should invalidate capital punishment of 16- and 17-year-old offenders on the ground that it fails to serve the legitimate goals of penology. According to petitioners, it fails to deter because juveniles, possessing less developed cognitive skills than adults, are less likely to fear death; and it fails to exact just retribution because juveniles, being less mature and responsible, are also less morally blameworthy. In support of these claims, petitioners and their supporting *amici* marshal an array of socioscientific evidence concerning the psychological and emotional development of 16- and 17-year-olds.

If such evidence could conclusively establish the entire lack of deterrent effect and moral responsibility, resort to the Cruel and Unusual Punishments Clause would be unnecessary; the Equal Protection Clause of the Fourteenth Amendment would invalidate these laws for lack of rational basis. . . . But as the adjective "socioscientific" suggests (and insofar as evaluation of moral responsibility is concerned perhaps the adjective "ethicoscientific" would be more apt), it is not demonstrable that no 16-year-old is "adequately responsible" or significantly deterred. It is rational, even if mistaken, to think the contrary. The battle must be

The Court improperly considered the law of foreign countries.

In coming to its decision in the Simmons case that juveniles cannot be executed, the Supreme Court's majority also erred by taking into consideration the laws of other nations. "Though

fought, then, on the field of the Eighth Amendment; and in that struggle socio-scientific, ethicoscientific, or even purely scientific evidence is not an available weapon. The punishment is either "cruel *and* unusual" (*i.e.,* society has set its face against it) or it is not. The audience for these arguments, in other words, is not this Court but the citizenry of the United States. It is they, not we, who must be persuaded. For as we stated earlier, our job is to *identify* the "evolving standards of decency"; to determine, not what they *should* be, but what they *are.* We have no power under the Eighth Amendment to substitute our belief in the scientific evidence for the society's apparent skepticism. In short, we emphatically reject petitioner's suggestion that the issues in this case permit us to apply our "own informed judgment," . . . regarding the desirability of permitting the death penalty for crimes by 16- and 17-year-olds. . . .

When this Court cast loose from the historical moorings consisting of the original application of the Eighth Amendment, it did not embark rudderless upon a wide-open sea. Rather, it limited the Amendment's extension to those practices contrary to the "evolving *standards* of decency that mark the progress of a maturing *society.*" . . . It has never been thought that this was a shorthand reference to the preferences of a majority of this Court. By reaching a decision supported neither by constitutional text nor by the demonstrable current standards of our citizens, the dissent displays a failure to appreciate that "those institutions which the Constitution is supposed to limit" include the Court itself. To say, as the dissent says, . . . that it is for *us* to judge, not on the basis of what we perceive the Eighth Amendment originally prohibited, or on the basis of what we perceive the society through its democratic processes now overwhelmingly disapproves, but on the basis of what we think "proportionate" and "measurably contributory to acceptable goals of punishment"—to say and mean that, is to replace judges of the law with a committee of philosopher-kings.

the views of our own citizens are essentially irrelevant to the Court's decision today, the views of other countries and the so-called international community take center stage," Scalia wrote in his dissent.[9] The Supreme Court, Scalia reasoned, is supposed to interpret American law, not international law or the laws of other nations. "More fundamentally, the basic premise of the

QUOTABLE

U.S. Supreme Court Associate Justice Antonin Scalia

In urging approval of a constitution that gave life-tenured judges the power to nullify laws enacted by the people's representatives, Alexander Hamilton assured the citizens of New York that there was little risk in this, since "[t]he judiciary . . . ha[s] neither FORCE nor WILL but merely judgment." . . . But Hamilton had in mind a traditional judiciary, "bound down by strict rules and precedents which serve to define and point out their duty in every particular case that comes before them." . . . Bound down, indeed. What a mockery today's opinion makes of Hamilton's expectation, announcing the Court's conclusion that the meaning of our Constitution has changed over the past 15 years—not, mind you, that this Court's decision 15 years ago was *wrong*, but that the Constitution *has changed*. The Court reaches this implausible result by purporting to advert, not to the original meaning of the Eighth Amendment, but to "the evolving standards of decency," . . . of our national society. It then finds, on the flimsiest of grounds, that a national consensus which could not be perceived in our people's laws barely 15 years ago now solidly exists. Worse still, the Court says in so many words that what our people's laws say about the issue does not, in the last analysis, matter: "[I]n the end our own judgment will be brought to bear on the question of the acceptability of the death penalty under the Eighth Amendment." . . . The Court thus proclaims itself sole arbiter of our Nation's moral standards—and in the course of discharging that awesome responsibility purports to take guidance from the views of foreign courts and legislatures. Because I do not believe that the meaning of our Eighth Amendment, any more than the meaning of other provisions of our Constitution, should be determined by the subjective views of five Members of this Court and like-minded foreigners, I dissent.

Source: *Roper v. Simmons*, 543 U.S. 551, 607-608 (J. Scalia, dissenting).

In this April 20, 2008 photo, U.S. Supreme Court Justice Antonin Scalia gives a lecture at the University of Virginia's law school in Charlottesville. Scalia, who believes the U.S. Constitution should trump rulemaking by judges, has been extremely critical of the Supreme Court's inconsistent rulings on the execution of minors.

Senate Resolution 92 (109th Congress)

Expressing the sense of the Senate that judicial determinations regarding the meaning of the Constitution of the United States should not be based on judgments, laws, or pronouncements of foreign institutions unless such foreign judgments, laws, or pronouncements inform an understanding of the original meaning of the Constitution of the United States.

Whereas the Declaration of Independence announced that one of the chief causes of the American Revolution was that King George had "combined with others to subject us to a jurisdiction foreign to our constitution, and unacknowledged by our laws";

Whereas the Supreme Court has recently relied on the judgments, laws, or pronouncements of foreign institutions to support its interpretations of the laws of the United States, most recently in *Atkins v. Virginia*, 536 U.S. 304, 316 n.21 (2002), *Lawrence v. Texas*, 539 U.S. 558, 573 (2003), and *Roper v. Simmons*, 125 S.Ct. 1183, 1198–99 (2005);

Whereas the Supreme Court has stated previously in *Printz v. United States*, 521 U.S. 898, 921 n.11 (1997), that "We think such comparative analysis inappropriate to the task of interpreting a constitution. . . .";

Whereas the ability of Americans to live their lives within clear legal boundaries is the foundation of the rule of law, and essential to freedom;

Whereas it is the appropriate judicial role to faithfully interpret the expression of the popular will through the Constitution and laws enacted by duly elected representatives of the American people and under our system of checks and balances;

Whereas Americans should not have to look for guidance on how to live their lives from the often contradictory decisions of any of hundreds of other foreign organizations; and

Whereas inappropriate judicial reliance on foreign judgments, laws, or pronouncements threatens the sovereignty of the United States, the separation of powers, and the President's and the Senate's treaty-making authority: Now, therefore, be it

Resolved, That it is the sense of the Senate that judicial interpretations regarding the meaning of the Constitution of the United States should not be based in whole or in part on judgments, laws, or pronouncements of foreign institutions unless such foreign judgments, laws, or pronouncements inform an understanding of the original meaning of the Constitution of the United States.

Source: http://cornyn.senate.gov/doc_archive/jc_other.S.Res.92.pdf.

Court's argument—that American law should conform to the laws of the rest of the world—ought to be rejected out of hand," he added.[10]

Summary

The U.S. Supreme Court has been unclear about where American law stands on the issue of the death penalty for juveniles. In 1989, the Court ruled 5–4 that it was constitutional to execute 16- and 17-year-old juvenile murderers. Then, in 2005, the Court ruled 5–4 that it was not constitutional to executive a 17-year-old murderer. Sadly, the Court's rulings in this area are unpredictable and could change yet again if the composition of the Supreme Court changes.

The Court should not establish a categorical rule that no juvenile murderer can be executed, since such a matter is an issue best left to individual state legislators. Several state attorneys general explained it well in their amicus brief to the Supreme Court in *Roper v. Simmons*: "A teenager who plots like an adult, kills like an adult, and covers up like an adult should be held responsible for his choices like an adult."[11]

Life Without Parole for Juveniles Is Unnecessary

Raphael Bernard Johnson committed what he calls a "hor-rible and senseless crime" as a 17-year-old juvenile. He shot and killed a young man after losing his temper at a party. Tried as an adult, he received a sentence of 10 to 25 years in prison. Fortunately, his sentence was not life in prison without the pos-sibility of parole. He felt he could be redeemed. "Because I had the chance of parole, a chance that thousands of young offenders serving life without parole do not have, I had hope," he told Con-gress years later, in 2008. "From day one [of his prison sentence] I saw the light at the end of the tunnel."[1] In prison, Johnson devoted himself to his rehabilitation by reading more than 1,300 books and earning certifications as a carpenter, plumber, electri-cian, and paralegal.[2]

After serving 12 years in prison, Johnson obtained release on parole and has become a model citizen. He graduated with honors from the University of Detroit Mercy, started his own company, published a book, and as of this writing works to help former offenders re-integrate into society.[3] He told Congress:

> I submit to you that everyone makes mistakes, errors in judgments and decisions that they wish they can take back at a later time. Perhaps this is especially true for young people. What I want to convey to you all is that for any juvenile offender who commits a crime as horrible and senseless as mine, there should still be some hope.[4]

Juveniles who receive life sentences without the possibility of parole do not have that light at the end of the tunnel. All they will see is a dark prison cell for the rest of their lives. Johnson's case shows why society should not give up on juveniles, even those convicted of murder.

Unfortunately, far too many juveniles receive life sentences without the possibility of parole and have no hope of ever seeing any light. More than 2,225 juveniles currently sit in prison in the United States and will never see the light of day because they have been sentenced to life without parole. More than 70 of those were only 13 or 14 when they committed their crimes.[5] "Imposing such a punishment contradicts our modern understanding that children have enormous potential for growth and maturity as they move from youth to adulthood, and the widely held belief in the possibility of a child's rehabilitation and redemption," write law professors Connie De La Vega and Michelle Leighton. "For many of the children who are sentenced to LWOP, it is effectively a death sentence carried out by the state over a long period of time."[6]

Life in prison amounts to a death sentence for juveniles.

Sentencing a young person to life in prison without the possibility of parole in effect condemns that minor to death. It offers no hope for rehabilitation but simply warehouses a person at great expense for many years. Elizabeth M. Calvin, a children's rights advocate for Human Rights Watch, explains: "The sentence of life without the possibility of parole is a sentence to die in prison.

Excerpts from the Equal Justice Initiative's Profiles of Dominic Culpepper and Ian Manuel

Dominic Culpepper—Florida

Dominic Culpepper suffered constant emotional and physical abuse from his mother, who beat him severely and told him she wished he was dead. Dominic's parents divorced and his father moved out, leaving him with his unstable and violent mother. Dominic was befriended by older men in the neighborhood who used him to deal drugs for them. When he was 14, a drug dealer who had threatened and stolen from Dominic came into his home. Dominic attacked him with a baseball bat. Afraid and confused, 14-year-old Dominic moved the injured drug dealer out of the house and contacted emergency services. Emergency services personnel were unable to save the young man's life and Dominic was arrested for murder. Although Dominic was only 14 and had used the bat against an intruder in his own home, the State of Florida sentenced him to die in prison.

Ian Manuel—Florida

Ian Manuel was raised in gruesome violence and extreme poverty. At age four, Ian was raped by a sibling. Violence and despair defined Ian's childhood and neighborhood and he was quickly pushed into destructive gang violence. When Ian was 13, he was directed by gang members to commit a robbery. During the botched robbery attempt, a woman suffered a nonfatal gunshot wound and a remorseful Ian turned himself in to the police. Ian's attorney instructed him to plead guilty and told him he would receive a 15-year sentence. Ian, accepting responsibility for his actions, pleaded guilty but was sentenced to life imprisonment without possibility of parole. Ian's lawyer never appealed or withdrew the plea. In prison, Ian has spent years in solitary confinement and repeatedly attempted suicide. The victim has forgiven Ian and petitioned for his release but the State of Florida demands that Ian remain in prison from the age of 13 until he is dead.

Source: http://www.eji.org/eji/files/20071017cruelandunusual.pdf.

There is no time off for good behavior. There is no chance to prove that you have become a different person. Next to the death penalty, there is no harsher condemnation."[7] In most instances, the law treats juveniles differently. Juveniles cannot serve in the military or drink alcohol or vote in political elections. Younger juveniles cannot drive a car or hold a job. Yet in many locales, a 14-year-old who cannot legally hold a job can be sentenced to life in prison without the possibility of parole. Something is seriously wrong with this picture.

Such life sentences are not rational or crime deterrents.

Life sentences for juveniles are bad policy and are not applied in a rational manner. While it might be necessary to give a juvenile with a long history of violent offenses a life sentence, particularly if rehabilitation efforts have repeatedly failed, all too often these life sentences are imposed on first-time offenders. Calvin explains that the Human Rights Watch estimates "that nationally 59 percent of youth who get this sentence are first-time offenders, without even a shoplifting on a criminal record."[8]

Even worse, many of these first-time juvenile offenders commit crimes under the influence or misguidance of adults. Unfortunately, nearly 60 percent of the time the adult offenders receive lighter sentences than the juveniles.[9] Similarly, these youths who receive such harsh sentences are often not the ringleaders of the crime. Calvin reports that "nearly half the youth sentenced to life without parole surveyed in Michigan were sentenced for aiding and abetting or for an unplanned murder that happened in the course of a felony."[10]

A common justification for stiff criminal penalties is that they will deter other individuals from perpetrating similar crimes. Young people, however, are not deterred from punishment nearly as much as adults because "they are less likely than adults to pause before acting, and when they do, research has failed to show that the threat of additional punishment deters them from crime."[11]

There are racial disparities among juveniles who receive life without parole sentences.

Another alarming problem with life sentences without parole concerns the presence of racial disparities, meaning that a disproportionate number of minorities receive such harsh sentences. "On average, across this country black youth are serving life without parole at a per capita rate that is 10 times that of white youth," Calvin testified before Congress. "Many states have racial disparities that are far greater than that."[12]

The Equal Justice Initiative reports that of the 73 13- and 14-year-olds sentenced to life in prison without parole in the United States, 49 percent are African-American. The group also reports that all of the 13- and 14-year-old juveniles in the United States sentenced to life without parole for nonhomicide

QUOTABLE

Bryan Stephenson

Young men of color, Muslim men, African-American men are presumed guilty [in the U.S. criminal justice system]. And so the lawyer has to overcome a presumption of guilt, which is not the way our system is set up, and as a result of that, lawyers fail to meet that burden. And we see that represented in the prison system. In this cohort of 13- and 14-year olds, all of the 13-year olds are Black. All of the kids who have been sentenced to die in prison at 13 and 14 for non-homicides are kids of color. All of them. And it reflects the way in which we can demonize and devalue and use race as a lens for that.

Source: Bryan Stephenson, speaking on the Juvenile Justice Accountability and Improvement Act of 2007 on September 11, 2008, to the House Subcommittee on Crime, Terrorism, and Homeland Security of the Committee of the Judiciary, H.R. 4300, 110th Cong., 2nd sess. U.S. Government Printing Office, 110-205, http://www.gpo.gov/fdsys/pkg/CHRG-110hhrg11044327/html/CHRG-110hhrg11044327.htm.

offenses have been children of color. These findings show, as the group reports, that "Children of Color Are Disproportionately Sentenced to Die in Prison."[13]

The international community condemns life imprisonment without parole for juveniles.

Although such harsh sentences for juveniles are routinely handed out in the United States, international law prohibits life without the possibility of parole sentences for juveniles. The United Nations' Convention on the Rights of the Child prohibits such punishments. Other countries around the globe condemn the punishment of life sentences without parole for juveniles; in fact, 135 countries explicitly reject this sentence in their laws.[14] For example, Germany rejects the traditional punishment model adopted in America for juvenile offenders. Instead, Germany focuses on rehabilitation. The maximum sentence for a child offender between the ages of 14 and 17 in that nation is five years in prison.[15]

At least two treaties to which the United States is a party also condemn the use of life sentences for juveniles. The enforcement bodies of two treaties to which the United States is a party, the International Covenant on Civil and Political Rights and the International Convention on the Elimination of All Forms of Racial Discrimination, have condemned such sentences.[16]

Scientific research supports lenient treatment for juveniles.

Various studes have found that there are key developmental differences between the brains of juveniles and those of adults. Simply stated, the brains of juveniles are not fully developed as compared with adults. In 2008, Dr. Richard G. Dudley Jr. told members of Congress that "children and adolescents do not yet have the physical brain capacity for the type of deci-sion-making we expect of adults and have legally held adults responsible for."[17]

Because children's brains are less developed, juveniles for the most part make fewer rational decisions. It also means that juveniles are not as morally culpable as adults because they have not yet developed a fully formed moral core. These technological advances in neuroscience have led many scientists to question the previously held assumption that brains are fully developed during childhood. As they are not, this should factor into pronouncing criminal sentences on juveniles.

International Resolutions Prohibiting Life Imprisonment for Juveniles

The Convention on the Rights of the Child
Article 37 (Detention and punishment): No one is allowed to punish children in a cruel or harmful way. Children who break the law should not be treated cruelly. They should not be put in prison with adults, should be able to keep in contact with their families, and should not be sentenced to death or life imprisonment without possibility of release.*

The Equal Justice Initiative
The International Covenant on Civil and Political Rights, to which the United States became a party in 1992, prohibits life without parole sentencing for juveniles. The official implementation body for the Convention Against Torture, Cruel, Inhuman or Degrading Treatment or Punishment commented that life imprisonment for children "could constitute cruel, inhuman or degrading treatment or punishment" in violation of the Convention. Further, the United Nations General Assembly passed by a 176–1 vote (the United States voted against) a resolution calling upon all nations to "abolish by law, as soon as possible, the death penalty and life imprisonment without possibility of release for those under the age of 18 years at the time of the commission of the offence."**

* The Convention on the Rights of the Child, http://www2.ohchr.org/english/law/pdf/crc.pdf.
**The Equal Justice Initiative, http://ap.ohchr.org/documents/E/HRC/resolutions/A_HRC_7_L_34.doc.

Sentencing children to life in prison subjects them to abuse.

Treating children as adults has another tragic dimension: It results in young people being sent to prison, sometimes in close contact with adults who can overpower them. The reality of prison rape and sexual abuse is a real and dangerous phenomenon imposed on these young people. As Bryan Stephenson, executive director of the Equal Justice Initiative, told Congress: "Yesterday I got a call from one of our young clients in Alabama, who was raped. We now assessed in our population of 13- and 14-year-olds that 70 percent have been victimized by sex crimes."[18]

Laws must be changed.

Tragically, sometimes state laws nearly force the hand of judges to approve of life sentences without the possibility of parole. That is because some mandatory sentencing laws require judges to impose a life sentence without considering age of the offender. Such laws must be amended, as the age of the offender should always be considered in sentencing. The California Court of Appeals correctly recognized this when it recently invalidated the conviction of Antonio Nunez, a 13-year-old sentenced to life in prison without the possibility of parole. The California court found that such a sentence violated its state constitution, writing: "Age also matters."[19]

There is a more sensible sentence for those juveniles who truly are violent and dangerous. Those juveniles could receive a life sentence *with* the possibility of parole. Professor Mark William Osler testified before a House subcommittee: "The child sentenced to life *with* the possibility of parole is still likely to perceive the weight of a nearly overwhelming punishment."[20]

Summary

The U.S. Supreme Court will decide whether life sentences for juveniles violate the Eighth Amendment's prohibition against "cruel and unusual punishment" in *Sullivan v. Florida* and

Graham v. Florida.[21] The case involves a life sentence imposed against Joe Sullivan, who was found guilty of having raped an elderly woman when he was 13 years old. "Florida is the *only state in the country* to have sentenced a thirteen-year-old child to die in prison for an offense in which the victim did not die, and Joe is the only thirteen-year-old in the country to have received such a sentence for sexual battery," his petition to the U.S. Supreme Court states.[22]

It is hoped the Supreme Court will invalidate life without parole for juvenile offenders in *Sullivan.* The sentence amounts to a death sentence and constitutes "cruel and unusual punishment" in violation of the Eighth Amendment. Such a sentence is not used in a rational fashion and is often applied in a racially disproportionate way that raises the specter of discrimination. Furthermore, scientific research confirms that juveniles simply do not appreciate the gravity of their actions as adults do and should not be subject to full-scale punitive treatment like adults. They should at least be given a chance to reform themselves. Even violent juvenile offenders should receive at most a life sentence *with* the possibility of parole.

Life Without Parole for Juveniles Is Necessary

In 2009, a 16-year-old boy allegedly raped a teenage girl in school. It turned out that this juvenile offender had previously been convicted of first-degree criminal sexual conduct at age 13.[1] In 2008, a 22-year-old allegedly killed a 17-year-old student and a 43-year-old woman and committed a spree of robberies. It turns out that the accused was a convicted sex offender who had been charged with 23 previous felonies, convicted of 23 misdemeanors, and had 18 probation violations.[2] In 2007, a 26-year-old man, who had had serious offenses as a juvenile, killed a police officer. When he was 16, he fired a gun at a classmate; at 17, he knifed a basketball player. Each time he received very lenient sentences. The result was that he was let back out to commit more crimes.[3]

Tragically, there are too many stories like these in which juveniles or young adults with violent criminal histories are allowed back on the street with what amounts to no more than a slap on the wrist. These juveniles were not amenable to the treatment they received in the juvenile justice system; in many cases, they were dangerous criminals who preyed on the public's sympathies to receive lighter sentences.

Certainly no one would argue that every juvenile should be sentenced to life in prison without the possibility of parole, although this penalty should be available for those who are found to be the worst of the worst. In Delaware, a 14-year-old defendant named Donald Torres received the sentence of life without parole. It is a very harsh sentence, but consider the harshness of the crime: Torres used kerosene to burn down his neighbor's house, knowing that a husband, wife, and two young children were asleep upstairs. Torres then watched as all four perished in the fire.[4]

The Supreme Court's decision in *Roper* is limited to the death penalty.

By a single vote (5–4), the U.S. Supreme Court ruled in *Roper v. Simmons* (2005) that sentencing a juvenile to death violates the Eighth Amendment's prohibition against "cruel and unusual punishment."[5] The Court's ruling, however, was specifically limited to the punishment of death. The U.S. Supreme Court has stated: "Death is different."[6] *Roper* does not—nor should it—extend to life without the possibility of parole.

In its *Roper* opinion, the U.S. Supreme Court specifically mentioned life without the possibility of parole as a possible alternative to the death penalty: "To the extent the juvenile death penalty might have residual deterrent effect, it is worth noting that the punishment of life imprisonment without the possibility of parole is itself a severe sanction, in particular for a young person."[7] The Court explained that life without the possibility of parole could be an effective deterrent or just as effective as the death penalty.

Lower courts have interpreted the Supreme Court's statement to mean that the Court considered its opinion in *Roper* to apply *only* to the death penalty. A Wisconsin appeals court upheld the life sentence without parole for Omer Ninham, who at age 14 killed a 13-year-old boy with others by throwing him over the fifth story of a parking garage.[8] The appeals court noted: "*Roper* does not support the proposition that a sentence to life without parole for acts committed by a fourteen-year-old is always inappropriate regardless of the depravity of the crime, the juvenile's character and the need to protect the public."[9]

The Connecticut Supreme Court rejected an Eighth Amendment claim by a juvenile convicted of murdering a fellow juvenile following a basketball game. The defendant argued that the Supreme Court's decision in *Roper* implied that life without parole was also cruel and unusual punishment and grossly disproportionate under the Eighth Amendment. The state's high court rejected that argument, noting that more than 40 states allowed life sentences without parole for juveniles. "The courts are in consensus, however, that the United States Supreme Court clearly has signaled that such a sentence does not violate the eighth amendment," the Connecticut Supreme Court wrote.

> The delineation between juveniles and adults for purposes of prosecution and punishment is a public policy determination reserved to the legislative branch of government, except where constitutional principles apply. The eighth amendment affords heightened significance to the "diminished culpability" of juveniles, but the reasoning of *Roper* does not extend to the present case.[10]

The sentence of life in prison without the possibility of parole "is not uncommon for a juvenile engaged in violent criminal activity, particularly where that juvenile is a recidivist [someone who reoffends]."[11] Other state courts have upheld such sentences. In 2008, the Ohio Supreme Court upheld the sentence for a 15-year-old juvenile who raped a 9-year-old girl.[12] In 2002, the South Carolina Supreme Court upheld a life sentence without parole for a 15-year-old juvenile who committed burglary and grand larceny. He received such a harsh sentence because he had previously been convicted of a serious felony. The court wrote that "lengthy sentences or sentences of life without parole upon juveniles do not violate contemporary standards of decency so as to constitute cruel and unusual punishment"[13] and "an enhanced sentence based upon a prior most serious *conviction* for a crime which was committed as a juvenile does not offend evolving standards of decency so as to constitute cruel and unusual punishment."[14]

Public safety must be the top priority.

Public safety demands that violent juvenile offenders, particularly those who have shown a penchant for re-offending, not be given slaps on the wrist. The number one priority of law enforcement in society is to protect the innocent from harm by wrongdoers. This requires that some violent juvenile offenders be taken off the street for good.

FROM THE BENCH

State v. Bunch (Ohio App. 2007)

The Supreme Court determines that it is unclear whether the death penalty provides a deterrent to juvenile offenders. It is at this point that the Supreme Court mentions life imprisonment without the possibility of parole. The purpose of mentioning life imprisonment without the possibility of parole is not to equate it with the death penalty. Rather, it is used to indicate that it is a severe sanction for a juvenile and due to the impact it has on a juvenile it could be used instead of the death penalty. It is simply indicating that life imprisonment without the possibility of parole is a good alternative to the death penalty for juveniles. It is not an indication that life imprisonment without the possibility of parole or an equivalent sentence to that is cruel and unusual punishment.

Violent juvenile crime has increased dramatically over the past 20 years. The Justice Department reported that the number of juvenile court cases involving serious offenses such as rape, robbery, aggravated assault, and murder skyrocketed an astonishing 68 percent between 1988 and 1992.[15] In 1996, Cook County, Illinois, state attorney Jack O'Malley said: "We've become a nation being terrorized by our children."[16] In an editorial written the same year for *U.S. News & World Report*, David Gergen summarized the problem in stark terms: "Evidence grows that we are spawning a new class of 'superpredators' who threaten far more mayhem in the next few years."[17] Although overall crime rates across the United States have decreased in recent years, juvenile crime continues to increase in certain cities across the country. In Nashville, Tennessee, for example, juvenile robbery statistics rose by 25 percent in 2007.[18]

Life without the possibility of parole does deter some juveniles.

Critics contend that life without the possibility of parole does not deter other would-be juvenile criminals. This ignores the commonsense reality that a life sentence—at the very least—deters the juvenile predator who committed murder by keeping him or her behind bars for good. It protects the public from someone who has proved to be dangerous.

Juvenile crime increased dramatically from the 1970s through much of the 1990s. In the 1990s, state legislators across the country addressed this epidemic by passing tougher laws that increased sentences for repeat juvenile offenders and for those juveniles who committed particularly egregious crimes. Juvenile crime began to drop in the late 1990s and the early 2000s. Many scholars would not like to admit this, but the stark reality is that the get-tough laws (also known as the "adult time for adult crime" laws) had an indelible effect and likely led to a reduction of harsh, violent juvenile crime. In other words, laws that provide for life without parole for juveniles deterred at least some would-be juvenile criminals from committing vicious crimes.

Removing life without the possibility of parole ignores victims' rights.

Much current legislation centers on the rights of those who committed criminal offenses. The system too often ignores the rights of those who lost loved ones at the hands of depraved young murderers. Jennifer Bishop-Jenkins knows too well what can happen with juvenile murderers. Her sister, brother-in-law, and

QUOTABLE

Jennifer Bishop-Jenkins

1. MYTH: That the real "problem" with the whole JLWOP [juvenile life without parole] situation is the age of the offender.

FACT: The real problem is that someone, or several someones are dead—murdered—and that an offender or offenders chose to commit acts of unspeakable evil against other innocent living human beings. And there is nothing but devastation in the wake of a murder.

What is at issue in all these cases are horrible, horrible murders and in all these cases tragedy surrounds the entire scenario. The problems go SO much deeper than just the age of the offender. Advocates against JLWOP need to do a much better job of embracing the full complexity of all these cases and talking about the CRIMES, not just the age of the offender. Reading their materials one could almost miss that these offenders are all convicted murderers, no matter what other circumstances surround the cases. . . .

3. MYTH: The offenders in these cases are CHILDREN.

FACT: 53% of all the offenders serving what these offenders called "juvenile life without parole" were 17 at the time of their offenses—hardly "children". And 17 in many states is the legal age of adulthood anyway.

The vast majority of the remaining (about 35%) were 16. Only the smallest numbers of cases—and the ones they of course love to publicize the most—

their soon-to-be born baby were murdered by a young man who wanted to go on a "thrill kill." As a result of that horror, Bishop-Jenkins founded the National Organization of Victims of Juvenile-Lifers. This group believes that certain juvenile offenders should not be released to wreak havoc on society again.

Summary

While many juveniles who commit minor crimes are capable of potential rehabilitation, some juveniles who commit horribly violent crimes are repeat offenders. For these repeat juvenile

were younger at the time of their offenses—single digit numbers. Legally every one of these offenders was found in a court or by state law to be legally an adult. Many states define adulthood at 17 or even 16. States vary on ages assigned for adult criminal culpability. . . .

5. **MYTH:** Many of the JLWOP cases are innocent of their crimes.
FACT: Most of the offenders serving JLWOP sentences are guilty of their crimes, and were the actual "trigger men", though some are convicted as direct accomplices with equal legal responsibility. A smaller percentage of the JLWOP cases were accomplices, serving life for felony murder counts.

But it is important to consider, if the proposal becomes to reform the felony murder counts for JLWOP, that there are actually some cases where accomplices could be seen as even more culpable than the "trigger men" if they directed or ordered the shooting, as is often the case in some gang killings.

In fact, any proposal that would lessen juvenile penalty for murder like this ACTUALLY ENDANGERS any potential juvenile offenders more because it will most certainly increase the number of older gang members who order the younger members to commit the crimes.

Source: Jennifer Bishop-Jenkins' written submission testimony before the House Subcommittee on Juvenile Justice, June 9, 2009, http://judiciary.house.gov/hearings/pdf/Jenkins090609.pdf.

offenders a sentence of life without the possibility of parole is the best option. The sentence does not violate the Eighth Amendment and constitute "cruel and unusual punishment." The U.S. Supreme Court has found that only the death penalty imposed on juveniles violates the Constitution. The majority of lower courts have rejected the extension of the Supreme Court's decision to life without parole.

Furthermore, life without parole for violent juveniles serves the primary goal of the criminal justice system: protecting the public. It also deters some would-be juvenile criminals. Finally, imposing this sentence also protects the rights of victims, people who are often too easily forgotten in the criminal process.

The Future of Juvenile Justice

Juvenile justice issues will never go away, and neither will the fundamental tension between the different schools of thought on the handling of delinquent youths. While some would emphasize the treatment options for delinquents, others advocate strong punishment. Juvenile justice will take center stage in the October 2009–June 2010 term of the U.S. Supreme Court, when the Court examines the constitutionality of life sentences without parole for juveniles in *Sullivan v. Florida*[1] and *Graham v. Florida*.[2] Both defendants were Florida juveniles sentenced to life in prison without any chance of parole. Sullivan was 13 when sentenced and Graham was 17.

Life imprisonment, however, is not the only juvenile justice issue that continues to raise tough questions. A continuing source of controversy concerns whether juvenile court records should be open to the public in a variety of circumstances. Some contend that there is a real danger in having too much secrecy regarding juvenile records.[3] For example, when an adult offender is prosecuted in criminal court, should prosecutors and the court have full access to the defendant's juvenile-court record? If there is no access to the defendant's juvenile-court record, a violent repeat offender would be considered a first-time offender in adult court when, in reality, the defendant has presented a threat to public safety for many years as a juvenile.[4]

Another pressing issue concerns the treatment of juvenile sex offenders. Many states have registration and community notification laws, which notify the public when a convicted sex offender has moved into a neighborhood. In some states, however, Randy Krebs writes, "there are no state mandates for informing communities including schools when juvenile predatory offenders are released back into society."[5]

Still another issue concerns juvenile treatment facilities. People vigorously disagree about the success rate of these treatment facilities. Are they too soft on hardened criminals or do they really work? Often, juvenile defendants escape from these treatment centers or boot camps, many of which do not have the same level of security as prisons. According to one report, there were eight escapes from the Albuquerque Boys Reintegration Center in New Mexico since it opened in December 2007.[6] There have even been escape attempts from extremely successful programs, such as the one at Giddings State Home and School in Texas.[7]

Congress continues to discuss proposed legislation dealing with a variety of juvenile justice issues. In the 111th Congress, the Juvenile Crime Reduction Act was introduced[8] as a measure that seeks to increase funding for treatment of juveniles' mental health and substance abuse disorders—problems that lead to much juvenile crime.

In the summer of 2009, the House Judiciary Committee held hearings on two other measures: the Juvenile Justice Accountability and Improvement Act of 2009[9] and the Youth

Teen boys march at a boot camp for juvenile offenders. The success of boot camps such as this one is much debated between those who believe that they are too lax for young criminals and those who think they help prevent juveniles from relapsing into criminal behavior.

Prison Reduction through Opportunity, Mentoring, Intervention, Support and Education Act.[10] Like the Juvenile Crime Reduction Act, these measures are aimed at helping juveniles in the criminal justice system.

Finally, another issue troubling to many concerns the pervasive influence of race in handing out stiff sentences to juveniles. Race considerations and allegations of discrimination permeate the criminal justice system. The juvenile justice system is no exception.[11]

In sum, juvenile justice remains an issue of the utmost importance in society. It affects the future of the country. In a

(continues on page 80)

Juvenile Crime Reduction Act of 2009, H.R. 1931

(1) USE OF FUNDS—The recipient of a grant awarded under this section shall use the funds to provide training, in conjunction with the public or private agency that provides mental health services, to individuals involved in making decisions regarding the disposition of cases involving youth who enter the juvenile justice system, including any of the following categories of individuals:

(A) Juvenile justice intake personnel.
(B) Law enforcement personnel.
(C) Prosecutors.
(D) Juvenile court judges.
(E) Public defenders.
(F) Mental health service providers and administrators.
(G) Substance abuse disorder service providers and administrators.
(H) Probation officers.
(I) Parents or parent advocates.

(2) FOCUS OF TRAINING—Training provided through a grant awarded under this section shall focus on the following:

(A) The availability of standardized, validated, age-appropriate, and culturally competent screening and assessment tools and the effective use of such tools to divert juveniles from secure confinement into home-based and community-based care.

(B) The purpose, benefits, and availability of home-based and community-based mental health or substance abuse treatment programs available to juveniles within the jurisdiction of the grantee.

(C) Public and private programs available to juveniles to pay for home-based and community-based mental health or substance abuse treatment programs.

(D) The appropriate use of effective home-based and community-based alternatives to juvenile justice or mental health system institutional placements. . . .

Source: H.R. 1931 (introduced April 2, 2009) (111th Congress), http://www.govtrack.us/congress/billtext.xpd?bill=h111-1931.

Juvenile Justice Accountability and Improvement Act of 2009

SECTION 1. SHORT TITLE.

This Act may be cited as the "Juvenile Justice Accountability and Improvement Act of 2009".

SEC. 2. FINDINGS.

Congress finds the following:

(1) Historically, courts in the United States have recognized the undeniable differences between adult and youth offenders.

(2) While writing for the majority in *Roper v. Simmons* (125 S. Ct. 1183), a recent Supreme Court decision abolishing use of the death penalty for juveniles, Justice Kennedy declared such differences to be "marked and well understood".

(3) Notwithstanding such edicts, many youth are being sentenced in a manner that has typically been reserved for adults. These sentences include a term of imprisonment of life without the possibility of parole.

(4) The decision to sentence youthful offenders to life without parole is an issue of growing national concern.

(5) While there are no youth serving such sentences in the rest of the world, research indicates that there are over 2,500 youth offenders serving life without parole in the United States.

(6) The estimated rate at which the sentence of life without parole is imposed on children nationwide remains at least 3 times higher today than it was 15 years ago.

(7) The majority of youth sentenced to life without parole are first-time offenders.

(8) Sixteen percent of these individuals were age 15 or younger when they committed their crimes.

SEC. 3. ESTABLISHING A MEANINGFUL OPPORTUNITY FOR PAROLE FOR CHILD OFFENDERS.

(a) In General—

(1) REQUIREMENTS—For each fiscal year after the expiration of the period specified in subsection (d)(1), each State shall have in effect laws and policies under which each child offender who is serving a life sentence receives, not

(continues)

(continued)

less than once during the first 15 years of incarceration, and not less than once every 3 years of incarceration thereafter, a meaningful opportunity for parole or other form of supervised release. This provision shall in no way be construed to limit the access of child offenders to other programs and appeals which they were rightly due prior to the enactment of this Act.

(2) REGULATIONS—Not later than 1 year after the date of the enactment of this Act, the Attorney General shall issue guidelines and regulations to interpret and implement this section.

Source: H.R. 2289 (introduced May 6, 2009) (111th Congress), http://www.govtrack.us/congress/billtext.xpd?bill=h111-2289.

(continued from page 77)

nation based on the rule of law, it is vitally important that the laws governing juvenile justice are fair and just, to society at large, the victims of juvenile crimes, and the juveniles themselves. Yet the controversy about finding the proper balance will continue, as various players—politicians, judges, public-interest groups, families of juvenile offenders, and families of crime victims—seek to treat young offenders with proper justice while protecting society. It is a precarious balance that has often teetered on different sides, depending on the political winds. The future of our country, however, hangs on a proper centering.

Beginning Legal Research

The goals of each book in the POINT/COUNTERPOINT series are not only to give the reader a basic introduction to a controversial issue affecting society, but also to encourage the reader to explore the issue more fully. This Appendix is meant to serve as a guide to the reader in researching the current state of the law as well as exploring some of the public policy arguments as to why existing laws should be changed or new laws are needed.

Although some sources of law can be found primarily in law libraries, legal research has become much faster and more accessible with the advent of the Internet. This Appendix discusses some of the best starting points for free access to laws and court decisions, but surfing the Web will uncover endless additional sources of information. Before you can research the law, however, you must have a basic understanding of the American legal system.

The most important source of law in the United States is the Constitution. Originally enacted in 1787, the Constitution outlines the structure of our federal government, as well as setting limits on the types of laws that the federal government and state governments can enact. Through the centuries, a number of amendments have added to or changed the Constitution, most notably the first 10 amendments, which collectively are known as the "Bill of Rights" and which guarantee important civil liberties.

Reading the plain text of the Constitution provides little information. For example, the Constitution prohibits "unreasonable searches and seizures" by the police. To understand concepts in the Constitution, it is necessary to look to the decisions of the U.S. Supreme Court, which has the ultimate authority in interpreting the meaning of the Constitution. For example, the U.S. Supreme Court's 2001 decision in *Kyllo v. United States* held that scanning the outside of a person's house using a heat sensor to determine whether the person is growing marijuana is an unreasonable search—if it is done without first getting a search warrant from a judge. Each state also has its own constitution and a supreme court that is the ultimate authority on its meaning.

Also important are the written laws, or "statutes," passed by the U.S. Congress and the individual state legislatures. As with constitutional provisions, the U.S. Supreme Court and the state supreme courts are the ultimate authorities in interpreting the meaning of federal and state laws, respectively. However, the U.S. Supreme Court might find that a state law violates the U.S. Constitution, and a state supreme court might find that a state law violates either the state or U.S. Constitution.

Not every controversy reaches either the U.S. Supreme Court or the state supreme courts, however. Therefore, the decisions of other courts are also important. Trial courts hear evidence from both sides and make a decision, while appeals courts review the decisions made by trial courts. Sometimes rulings from appeals courts are appealed further to the U.S. Supreme Court or the state supreme courts.

Lawyers and courts refer to statutes and court decisions through a formal system of citations. Use of these citations reveals which court made the decision or which legislature passed the statute, and allows one to quickly locate the statute or court case online or in a law library. For example, the Supreme Court case *Brown v. Board of Education* has the legal citation 347 U.S. 483 (1954). At a law library, this 1954 decision can be found on page 483 of volume 347 of the U.S. Reports, which are the official collection of the Supreme Court's decisions. On the following page, you will find samples of all the major kinds of legal citation.

Finding sources of legal information on the Internet is relatively simple thanks to "portal" sites such as findlaw.com and lexisone.com, which allow the user to access a variety of constitutions, statutes, court opinions, law review articles, news articles, and other useful sources of information. For example, findlaw.com offers access to all Supreme Court decisions since 1893. Other useful sources of information include gpo.gov, which contains a complete copy of the U.S. Code, and thomas.loc.gov, which offers access to bills pending before Congress, as well as recently passed laws. Of course, the Internet changes every second of every day, so it is best to do some independent searching.

Of course, many people still do their research at law libraries, some of which are open to the public. For example, some state governments and universities offer the public access to their law collections. Law librarians can be of great assistance, as even experienced attorneys need help with legal research from time to time.

Common Citation Forms

Source of Law	Sample Citation	Notes
U.S. Supreme Court	*Employment Division v. Smith*, 485 U.S. 660 (1988)	The U.S. Reports is the official record of Supreme Court decisions. There is also an unofficial Supreme Court ("S. Ct.") reporter.
U.S. Court of Appeals	*United States v. Lambert*, 695 F.2d 536 (11th Cir.1983)	Appellate cases appear in the Federal Reporter, designated by "F." The 11th Circuit has jurisdiction in Alabama, Florida, and Georgia.
U.S. District Court	*Carillon Importers, Ltd. v. Frank Pesce Group, Inc.*, 913 F.Supp. 1559 (S.D.Fla.1996)	Federal trial-level decisions are reported in the Federal Supplement ("F. Supp."). Some states have multiple federal districts; this case originated in the Southern District of Florida.
U.S. Code	Thomas Jefferson Commemoration Commission Act, 36 U.S.C., §149 (2002)	Sometimes the popular names of legislation—names with which the public may be familiar—are included with the U.S. Code citation.
State Supreme Court	*Sterling v. Cupp*, 290 Ore. 611, 614, 625 P.2d 123, 126 (1981)	The Oregon Supreme Court decision is reported in both the state's reporter and the Pacific regional reporter.
State Statute	Pennsylvania Abortion Control Act of 1982, 18 Pa. Cons. Stat. 3203-3220 (1990)	States use many different citation formats for their statutes.

Cases

Kent v. United States, 383 U.S. 541 (1966)
In this decision, the U.S. Supreme Court ruled that juvenile courts must have certain level of procedural protections in place before transferring a juvenile to adult criminal court.

In Re Gault, 387 U.S. 1 (1967)
In this decision, the U.S. Supreme Court ruled that juvenile court defendants are entitled to many of the same constitutional protections as adults. For example, the Court ruled that juveniles are entitled to a level of due process.

In Re Winship, 397 U.S. 358 (1970)
In this decision, the U.S. Supreme Court ruled that the adult criminal law evidentiary standard of "beyond a reasonable doubt" is applicable and required in juvenile court proceedings.

McKeiver v. Pennsylvania, 403 U.S. 528 (1971)
In this decision, the U.S. Supreme Court ruled that juveniles are not entitled to jury trials in juvenile court proceedings.

Stanford v. Kentucky, 492 U.S. 361 (1989)
In this decision, the U.S. Supreme Court ruled 5–4 that a state could execute 16- or 17-year-old murderers. The Court noted that many states allowed such executions. The Court overruled this decision in *Roper v. Simmons*.

Roper v. Simmons, 543 U.S. 551 (2005)
In this decision, the U.S. Supreme Court ruled 5–4 that executing juveniles violated the Eighth Amendment's prohibition against "cruel and unusual punishment." The Court reasoned that juveniles are less culpable than adults. In reaching its decision, the Court considered the law of other countries, in addition to U.S. law.

Terms and Concepts

Aggravating factors

Blended sentencing

Delinquent

Deterrence

Due process

Eighth Amendment

Evolving standards of decency

Life sentence

Mitigating factors

Parole

Rehabilitation

Sentencing

Terms and Concepts *(continued)*
Transfer
Victims' rights
Waiver

Introduction: An Overview of Juvenile Justice

1 Quoted in F.M.B., "The Youthful Delinquent: A New Way to Deal with Him," *New York Times*, February 25, 1906.
2 Steven Mintz, *Huck's Raft: A History of American Childhood* (Cambridge, Mass.: Belknap Press of Harvard University Press, 2004), 176.
3 "Politics Blasts Founders' Aims for St. Charles," *Chicago Daily Tribune*, February 15, 1941.
4 F.M.B., "The Youthful Delinquent: A New Way to Deal with Him," *New York Times*.
5 "The Juvenile Court," *Atlanta Constitution*, September 20, 1904.
6 Quoted in "Colorado Judge Talks of Boys," *Los Angeles Times*, February 29, 1904.
7 Ibid.
8 Mintz, *Huck's Raft*, 177.
9 Ibid.
10 Mintz, *Huck's Raft*, 178.
11 Quoted in "Says Juvenile Court Upholds Child Rights: Judge Goldsmith at Syracuse Tells of Advance," *New York Times*, December 10, 1933.
12 "Politics Blasts Founders' Aims for St. Charles," *Chicago Daily Tribune*.
13 *Kent v. United States*, 383 U.S. 541, 554 (1966).
14 Ibid., 554.
15 *In Re Gault*, 387 U.S. 1 (1967).
16 Ibid., 28.
17 *In Re Winship*, 397 U.S. 358 (1970).
18 *McKeiver v. Pennsylvania*, 403 U.S. 528 (1971).
19 Nathaniel Sheppard Jr. and William Reckenwald, "New Upsurge in Street Gangs: Crime, Violent Activity Increase in City and Suburbs," *Chicago Tribune*, January 8, 1994.
20 John Hubner, *Last Chance in Texas: The Redemption of Criminal Youth* (New York: Random House, 2008), xix.
21 *Stanford v. Kentucky*, 492 U.S. 937 (1989).
22 *Roper v. Simmons*, 543 U.S. 551 (2005).

Point: Juveniles Should Not Be Treated as Adults

1 Benjamin Steiner and Emily Wright, "Assessing the Relative Effects of State Direct File Waiver Laws on Violent Juvenile Crime: Deterrence or Irrelevance?" 96 *Journal of Criminal Law & Criminology* 1451, 1467 (2006).
2 David Ress, "Tough Juvenile Crime Laws Get Second Look," *Richmond Times Dispatch* (Va.), December 2, 2007.
3 Kelly M. Angell, "The Regressive Movement: When Juvenile Offenders Are Treated as Adults, Nobody Wins," 14 *Southern California Interdisciplinary Law Journal* 125, 132 (2004).
4 Emily A. Polachek, "Juvenile Transfer: From 'Get Better' to 'Get Tough' and Where We Go From Here," 35 *William Mitchell Law Review* 1162, 1169 (2009).
5 Ibid.
6 Angell, "The Regressive Movement," 135.
7 Sharon Cohen, Associated Press, "Studies Indicate Sending Kids to Adult Courts May Be Counterproductive," December 1, 2007.
8 Task Force on Community Preventive Services, "Effects on Violence of Laws and Policies Facilitating the Transfer of Youth from the Juvenile to the Adult Justice System," November 30, 1997. Available online. URL: http://www.cdc.gov/mmwr/PDF/rr/rr5609.pdf.
9 Ibid.
10 Ibid.
11 Ibid., 7.
12 Ibid., 10.
13 Greg Mathis, "Trying Juveniles as Adults Doesn't Work," *Miami Times*, May 30, 2007.
14 Polachek, "Juvenile Transfer," 1177.
15 Building Blocks for Youths, "Children in Adult Jail, Factsheet." Available online. URL: http://www.buildingblocksforyouth.org/issues/adultjails/factsheet.html.

16 Angell, "The Regressive Movement," 143.

17 Steiner and Wright, "Assessing the Relative Effects of State Direct File Waiver Laws on Violent Juvenile Crime," 1467.

18 Ibid., 1469.

19 Steven A. Dirzin and Greg Luloff, "Are Juvenile Courts A Breeding Ground for Wrongful Convictions?" 34 *Northern Kentucky Law Review* 257 (2007).

20 Barry Feld, "A Century of Juvenile Justice: A Work in Progress or a Revolution that Failed?" 34 *Northern Kentucky Law Review* 189, 223–224 (2007).

21 Polachek, "Juvenile Transfer," 1177.

22 Ibid. 1182.

23 Mathis, "Trying Juveniles as Adults Doesn't Work."

Counterpoint: Some Juveniles Should Be Treated as Adults

1 Joseph Neff, "Court System Failed to Curb Lovette; Officials Didn't Act to Rein in the Teen Despite His History of Intensifying Criminal Behavior," *News & Observer* (Raleigh, N.C.), April 4, 2008.

2 Durham District Attorney David Saacks, quoted in Neff, "Court System Failed to Curb Lovette."

3 Benjamin Adams and Sean Addie, "Delinquency Cases Waived to Criminal Court, 2005," OJJDP Fact Sheet, June 2009, 1. Available online. URL: http://www.ncjrs.gov/pdffiles1/ojjdp/224539.pdf.

4 Task Force on Community Preventive Services, "Effects on Violence of Laws and Policies Facilitating the Transfer of Youth from the Juvenile to the Adult Justice System," November 30, 2007, 2. Available online. URL: http://www.cdc.gov/mmwr/PDF/rr/rr5609.pdf.

5 Adams and Addie, "Delinquency Cases Waived to Criminal Court, 2005," 1.

6 Burns Indiana Code Ann. § 31-30-3-2.

7 Oregon Revised Statutes § 419C.349 (2007).

8 National Center for Juvenile Justice, "Which States Have Blended Sentencing Laws?" Available online. URL: http://www.ncjj.org/stateprofiles/overviews/faqbs.asp.

9 Ibid.

10 Kristin L. Cabarello, "Blended Sentencing: A Good Idea for Juvenile Sex Offenders," 19 *St. John's Journal of Legal Commentary* 379, 413 (2005).

11 John Hubner, *Last Chance in Texas: The Redemption of Criminal Youth* (New York: Random House, 2008), 86.

12 Ibid., 87.

13 Robert Sexton, "Old Enough to Kill; Few Violent Juveniles Ever Make It to Adult Court," *Daily News of Los Angeles*, May 18, 1997.

14 James Fox, testifying on H.R. 2289, the Juvenile Justice Accountability and Improvement Act of 2009, on June 9, 2009, to the House Judiciary Subcommittee on Crime, Terrorism, and Homeland Security hearing. Available online. URL: http://judiciary.house.gov/hearings/pdf/Fox090609.pdf.

15 Sexton, "Old Enough to Kill."

16 Sam Vincent Meddis, "Poll: Treat Juveniles the Same as Adult Offenders," *USA Today*, October 29, 1993.

17 Thomas A. Vonder Haar, "A Free Ride for Juvenile Offenders," *St. Louis Post-Dispatch*, May 2, 1995.

18 Julie Ray, "Public: Adult Crimes Require Adult Time," Gallup.com, November 15, 2003. Available online. URL: http://www.gallup.com/poll/9682/public-adult-crimes-require-adult-time.aspx.

Point: Juveniles Should Not Receive the Death Penalty

1 Patricia Smith, "Brenton Butler Didn't Do It: But He Did Confess," *New York Times*, September 1, 2003.

2 Hugh Dellios, "Youth Guilty in Assault, Murder of Med Student," *Chicago Tribune*, February 10, 1998.

3 Steve Mills, "3 Roscetti Inmates Walk Free; After 15 Years, New World Greets Them as Judge Tosses Convictions," *Chicago Tribune*, December 6, 2001.

4 Ibid.

5 Bennie Currie, "Chicago City Council Settles $1.5 Million Lawsuit Over Wrongful Conviction," Associated Press, July 29, 2003.

6 Jeff Coen, "Guilty Pleas Close a 'Horrible Saga'; 2 Admit Roles in 1986 Murder of Lori Roscetti," *Chicago Tribune*, December 17, 2004.

7 *Gregg v. Georgia*, 428 U.S. 153, 188 (1976).

8 *Furman v. Georgia*, 408 U.S. 238 (1972).

9 Ibid., 309 (J. Stewart, concurring).

10 *Ford v. Wainwright*, 477 U.S. 399 (1986).

11 *Atkins v. Virginia*, 536 U.S. 304 (2002).

12 *Thompson v. Oklahoma*, 487 U.S. 815 (1988).

13 *Stanford v. Kentucky*, 492 U.S. 361 (1989).

14 *Trop v. Dulles*, 356 U.S. 86, 101 (1958).

15 Ibid.

16 David L. Hudson Jr., "Does Capital Punishment Have a Future?: A Resource Guide for Teachers," American Bar Association (2004), 18.

17 Ibid., 16.

18 *Roper v. Simmons*, 543 U.S. 551 (2005).

19 *Stanford*, 361.

20 *Roper*, 569–570.

21 Ibid., 570.

22 Ibid., 575.

23 Amicus brief of Coalition for Juvenile Justice, *Roper v. Simmons* (03-633), 8.

24 Ibid., 14–15.

25 Amicus brief of American Bar Association, *Roper v. Simmons* (03-633), 13. Available online. URL: http://www.abanet.org/crimjust/juvjus/simmons/aba.pdf.

26 Ibid.

Counterpoint: Some Older Juveniles Should Receive the Death Penalty

1 *Roper v. Simmons*, 543 U.S. 551, 600 (2005) (J. O'Connor, dissenting).

2 Ibid.

3 Ibid., 601.

4 *Stanford v. Kentucky*, 492 U.S. 361, 365 (1989).

5 Ibid., 366.

6 Ibid., 371.

7 Amicus brief of Justice for All Alliance in support of Petitioner, *Roper v. Simmons* (03-633), 20–21.

8 *Roper v. Simmons*, 543 U.S. 551, 601 (J. O'Connor, dissenting).

9 *Roper v. Simmons*, 543 U.S. 551, 622 (J. Scalia, dissenting).

10 Ibid., 624.

11 Amicus brief of the states of Alabama, Delaware, Oklahoma, Texas, Utah, and Virginia, in support of Petitioner, *Roper v. Simmons* (03-633), 14.

Point: Life Without Parole for Juveniles Is Unnecessary

1 Raphael B. Johnson, speaking on the Juvenile Justice Accountability and Improvement Act of 2007 on September 11, 2008, to the House Subcommittee on Crime, Terrorism, and Homeland Security of the Committee of the Judiciary, H.R. 4300, 110th Cong., 2nd sess., U.S. Government Printing Office, 110-205, 52. Available online. URL: http://judiciary.house.gov/hearings/printers/110th/44327.pdf.

2 Ibid., 52–53.

3 Ibid., 53.

4 Ibid.

5 Equal Justice Initiative, "Cruel and Unusual: Sentencing 13- and 14-Year Old Children to Die in Prison," November 2007. Available online. URL: http://eji.org/eji/files/20071017cruelandunusual.pdf.

6 Connie De La Vega and Michelle Leighton, "Sentencing Our Children to Die in Prison: Global Law

and Practice," 42 *University of San Francisco Law Review* 983, 983–984 (2008).

7 Elizabeth M. Calvin, speaking on the Juvenile Justice Accountability and Improvement Act of 2007 on September 11, 2008, to the House Subcommittee on Crime, Terrorism, and Homeland Security of the Committee of the Judiciary, H.R. 4300, 110th Cong., 2nd sess., U.S. Government Printing Office, 110-205, 59. Available online. URL: http://judiciary.house.gov/hearings/printers/110th/44327.pdf.

8 Ibid., 59.

9 Ibid., 60.

10 Ibid.

11 Ibid., 65.

12 Ibid., 60.

13 Equal Justice Initiative, "Cruel and Unusual," 21.

14 De La Vega and Leighton, "Sentencing Our Children to Die in Prison," 989.

15 Ibid., 1019.

16 Calvin, testimony to House subcommittee, 65.

17 Dr. Richard G. Dudley Jr., speaking on the Juvenile Justice Accountability and Improvement Act of 2007 on September 11, 2008, to the House Subcommittee on Crime, Terrorism, and Homeland Security of the Committee of the Judiciary, H.R. 4300, 110th Cong., 2nd sess., U.S. Government Printing Office, 110-205, 28. Available online. URL: http://judiciary.house.gov/hearings/printers/110th/44327.pdf.

18 Bryan Stephenson, speaking on the Juvenile Justice Accountability and Improvement Act of 2007 on September 11, 2008, to the House Subcommittee on Crime, Terrorism, and Homeland Security of the Committee of the Judiciary, H.R. 4300, 110th Cong., 2nd sess., U.S. Government Printing Office, 110-205, 13. Available online. URL: http://judiciary.house.

gov/hearings/printers/110th/44327.pdf.

19 *In Re Nunez*, 173 Cal.App.4th 709, 726 (Cal.App. 2009).

20 Professor Mark William Osler, speaking on the Juvenile Justice Accountability and Improvement Act of 2009 on June 9, 2009, to the House Subcommittee on Crime, Terrorism, and Homeland Security, H.R. 2289. Available online. URL: http://judiciary.house.gov/hearings/pdf/Osler090609.pdf.

21 *Sullivan v. Florida* (08-7621), *Graham v. Florida* (08-7412).

22 Petition for Writ of Certiorari, *Sullivan v. Florida* (08-7621), 28.

Counterpoint: Life Without Parole for Juveniles Is Necessary

1 Randy Krebs, "Laws Must Be Altered for Safety," *St. Cloud Times* (Minn.), April 18, 2009.

2 "For the Public's Sake, Repeat Juvenile Offenders Need More Than Mercy," *Wilmington News Journal*, October 20, 2008.

3 Michelle McPhee, " 'Laxachusetts': Where Criminals Get Coddled," *Boston Herald*, December 3, 2007.

4 *Torres v. State*, 972 A.2d 312 (De. 2009).

5 *Roper v. Simmons*, 543 U.S. 551 (2005).

6 *Gregg v. Georgia*, 428 U.S. 153, 188 (1976).

7 Ibid., 572.

8 *State v. Ninham*, No. 2008AP1139 (Wis. App.) (March 3, 2009).

9 Ibid., 82.

10 *State v. Allen*, 958 A.2d 1214, 1236 (Conn. 2008).

11 Respondent's Brief in Opposition, *Graham v. Florida* (08-7412), 16.

12 *State v. Warren*, 887 N.E.2d 1145 (Ohio 2008).

13 *State v. Standard*, 569 S.E.2d 325, 329 (S.C. 2002).

14 Ibid.

NOTES ⫸

15 Joseph Perkins, "Nation's Young Criminals Deserve Adult Punishment," *Rocky Mountain News*, August 3, 1994.

16 Quoted in Peter Annin, " 'Superpredators' Alive," *Newsweek*, January 22, 1996, 57.

17 David Gergen, "Taming Teenage Wolf Packs," *U.S. News & World Report*, March 25, 1996, 68.

18 Kate Howard, "DA Says Try More Kids as Adults," *Tennessean* (Nashville), December 17, 2008.

Conclusion: The Future of Juvenile Justice

1 *Sullivan v. Florida* (08-7621).

2 *Graham v. Florida* (08-7412).

3 John Schwade, "The Danger of Too Much Secrecy on Juvenile Records," *News & Observer* (Raleigh, N.C.), April 19, 2008.

4 Ibid.

5 Randy Krebs, "Laws Must Be Altered for Safety," *St. Cloud Times* (Minn.), April 18, 2008.

6 Susie Gran, "Eight Escapes in One Year: Critics Seek Increased Security for Teenagers in State Custody," *Albuquerque Tribune* (N.M.), February 4, 2008.

7 Mike Ward, "Plan Would Put Violent Teens in Adult Jails; After Giddings Escape, Plan Aims to Put Violent Teens in Adult Jails," *Austin American-Statesman* (Texas), November 14, 1996.

8 H.R. 1931, Juvenile Crime Reduction Act.

9 H.R. 2289 (111th Cong.) Juvenile Justice Accountability and Improvement Act of 2009.

10 H.R. 1064 (111th Cong.) Youth Prison Reduction through Opportunity, Mentoring, Intervention, Support and Education Act.

11 John Hubner, *Last Chance in Texas: The Redemption of Criminal Youth* (New York: Random House, 2008), 227–229.

Books and Articles

Angell, Kelly M., "The Regressive Movement: When Juvenile Offenders Are Treated as Adults, Nobody Wins," 14 *Southern California Interdisciplinary Law Journal* 125 (2004).

Beresford, Lisa S., "Is Lowering the Age at Which Juveniles Can Be Transferred to Adult Criminal Court the Answer to Juvenile Crime? A State-by-State Assessment," 37 *San Diego Law Review* 783 (2000).

Bishop, Donna M., Charles E. Frazier, Lonn Lanza-Kaduce, and Lawrence Winner, "The Transfer of Juveniles to Criminal Court: Does It Make a Difference?" 42 *Crime & Delinquency* 171 (1996).

Cabarello, Kristin L., "Blended Sentencing: A Good Idea for Juvenile Sex Offenders," 19 *St. John's Journal of Legal Commentary* 379 (2005).

De La Vega, Connie, and Michelle Leighton, "Sentencing Our Children to Die in Prison: Global Law and Practice," 42 *University of San Francisco Law Review* 983 (2008).

Dirzin, Steven A., and Greg Luloff, "Are Juvenile Courts A Breeding Ground for Wrongful Convictions?" 34 *Northern Kentucky Law Review* 257 (2007).

Equal Justice Initiative, "Cruel and Unusual: Sentencing 13- and 14-Year Old Children to Die in Prison," (2008). Available online. URL: http://eji. org/eji/files/20071017cruelandunusual.pdf.

Feld, Barry, "Abolish the Juvenile Court: Youthfulness, Criminal Responsibility, and Sentencing Policy," 88 *Journal of Criminal Law & Criminology* 68 (1997).

———. "A Century of Juvenile Justice: A Work in Progress or a Revolution that Failed?" 34 *Northern Kentucky Law Review* 189 (2007).

———. "Criminalizing the American Juvenile Court," 17 *Crime & Justice* 197 (1993).

Fox, Sanford J., "Juvenile Justice Reform: An Historical Perspective," 22 *Stanford Law Review* 1187 (1969).

Hubner, John, *Last Chance in Texas: The Redemption of Criminal Youth* (New York: Random House, 2008).

Hudson, David L. Jr., "Does Capital Punishment Have a Future: A Resource Guide for Teachers," American Bar Association, Division for Public Education, Chicago, 2004.

————. "Race, Ethnicity, and the American Criminal Justice System," American Bar Association, Division for Public Education, Chicago, 2005.

Humes, Edward, *No Matter How Loud I Shout: A Year in the Life of Juvenile Court* (New York: Simon & Schuster, 1997).

Kaban, Barbara, and Anne Tobey, "When Police Question Children: Are Protections Adequate?" 1 *Judicial Center for Children & Courts* 151 (1999).

Klein, Eric K., "Dennis the Menace or Billy the Kid: An Analysis of the Role of Transfer to Criminal Court in Juvenile Justice," 35 *American Criminal Law Review* 371 (1998).

Mack, Julian W., "The Juvenile Court," 23 *Harvard Law Review* 104 (1909).

Moore, Mark H., and Stewart Wakeling, "Juvenile Justice: Shoring Up the Foundations," 22 *Crime & Justice* 253 (1997).

Park, Jennifer, "Balancing Rehabilitation and Punishment: A Legislative Solution for Unconstitutional Juvenile Waiver Policies," 76 *George Washington Law Review* 786 (2008).

Polachek, Emily A., "Juvenile Transfer: From 'Get Better' to 'Get Tough' and Where We Go From Here," 35 *William Mitchell Law Review* 1162 (2009).

Scott, Elizabeth S., and Thomas Grisso, "The Evolution of Adolescence: A Developmental Perspective on Juvenile Justice Reform," 88 *Journal of Criminal Law & Criminology* 137 (1998).

Shefi, Ellie D., "Waiving Goodbye: Incarcerating Waived Juveniles in Adult Correctional Facilities Will Not Reduce Crime," 36 *University of Michigan Journal of Legal Reform* 653 (2003).

Steiner, Benjamin, and Emily Wright, "Assessing the Relative Effects of State Direct File Waiver Laws on Violent Juvenile Crime: Deterrence or Irrelevance?" 96 *Journal of Criminal Law & Criminology* 1451 (2006).

Task Force on Community Preventive Services, "Effects on Violence of Laws and Policies Facilitating the Transfer of Youth from the Juvenile to the Adult Justice System," Centers for Disease Control and Prevention, November 30, 2007.

Thomas, Charles W., and Shay Bilchik, "Prosecuting Juveniles in Criminal Courts: A Legal and Empirical Analysis," 76 *Journal of Criminal Law & Criminology* 439 (1985).

Yeckel, Joseph, "Violent Juvenile Offenders: Rethinking Federal Intervention in Juvenile Justice," 51 *Washington University Journal Urban & Contemporary Law* 331 (1997).

Web Sites

ACLU—Children's Rights
http://www.aclu.org/intlhumanrights/childrensrights/39380res20090609.html
The American Civil Liberties Union Web site criticizes the practice of sentencing juveniles to life imprisonment without parole.

American Bar Association's Juvenile Justice Committee
http://www.abanet.org/crimjust/juvjus/
According to its Web site, the Juvenile Justice Committee of the ABA Criminal Justice Section maintains "an active voice in promoting changes in the juvenile justice system. The Committee is an interdisciplinary forum of defenders, judges, prosecutors, corrections staff, law students, and others interested in improving the juvenile justice system for kids, parents, and the professionals who serve them."

Building Blocks for Youth
http://www.buildingblocksforyouth.org/
Building Blocks for Youth, according to its Web site, is "an alliance of children and youth advocates, researchers, law enforcement professionals and community organizers that seeks to: 1) Reduce overrepresentation and disparate treatment of youth of color in the justice system; 2) Promote fair, rational and effective juvenile justice policies."

Coalition for Juvenile Justice
http://www.juvjustice.org/
As described on its Web site, this nonprofit organization's mission "is to build safe communities one child at a time by ensuring that all children and families are treated fairly and given the resources and support to be positive and productive contributors to society."

Office of Juvenile Justice and Delinquency Prevention (OJJDP)

http://ojjdp.ncjrs.org/

According to its Web site, this federal agency (which is a component of the Office of Justice Programs in the U.S. Department of Justice) "accomplishes its mission by supporting states, local communities, and tribal jurisdictions in their efforts to develop and implement effective programs for juveniles. The Office strives to strengthen the juvenile justice system's efforts to protect public safety, hold offenders accountable, and provide services that address the needs of youth and their families."

PICTURE CREDITS

DAVID L. HUDSON JR. is a First Amendment Scholar at the First Amendment Center at Vanderbilt University. He teaches law classes at Middle Tennessee State University, Nashville School of Law, and Vanderbilt Law School. He is the author or co-author of more than 20 books, including several in the POINT/COUNTERPOINT series.

ALAN MARZILLI, M.A., J.D., lives in Birmingham, Ala., and is a program associate with Advocates for Human Potential, Inc., a research and consulting firm based in Sudbury, Mass., and Albany, N.Y. He primarily works on developing training and educational materials for agencies of the federal government on topics such as housing, mental health policy, employment, and transportation. He has spoken on mental health issues in 30 states, the District of Columbia, and Puerto Rico; his work has included training mental health administrators, nonprofit management and staff, and people with mental illnesses and their families on a wide variety of topics, including effective advocacy, community-based mental health services, and housing. He has written several handbooks and training curricula that are used nationally—as far away as the territory of Guam. He managed statewide and national mental health advocacy programs and worked for several public interest lobbying organizations while studying law at Georgetown University. He has written more than a dozen books, including numerous titles in the POINT/COUNTERPOINT series.